Monday Morning
Mentoring

Other Books by David Cottrell:

Monday Morning
Mentoring

Ten Lessons
to Guide You Up the Ladder

David Cottrell

Collins
An Imprint of HarperCollins*Publishers*

HarperCollins books may be purchased for educational, business, or sales
promotional use. For information, please write to: Special Markets
Department, HarperCollins Publishers, 10 East 53rd Street, New York,
NY 10022.

Designed by William Ruoto

Library of Congress Cataloging-in-Publication has been applied for.

ISBN-13: 978-0-06-088822-0
ISBN-10: 0-06-088822-9

06 07 08 09 10 / 10 9 8 7 6 5 4 3 2 1

This book is dedicated to those who have the courage to learn, the vision to lead, and the passion to share.

Contents

Prologue

Two years ago . . .

My life was not going well.

For several years, I had been a relatively successful manager for a Fortune 500 company, but now I was in a slump. I was working harder than ever but going nowhere. I barely saw my kids, my marriage was suffering, and my health was not the best.

I was struggling in every part of my life.

At work, my team also was feeling the effects of my slump. Tension was high, some people had reached their breaking points, and business was slow—real slow. The pressure to improve performance was rapidly hitting the "unbearable" level, and, to be honest, I was ready to give up . . . mainly because my doubts about my leadership abilities were overwhelming the confidence I once had.

My questions outnumbered my answers. What if I

were no longer the right person for a leadership position? What if I had been successful in the past because of the great economy . . . or just extremely lucky?

I was at a loss.

Exhausting my own resources, now I needed to talk to someone—someone who would listen and offer suggestions without judging me. I had become negative and had a hard time believing anybody really cared about me or my problems at work and at home.

One Saturday on the golf course, I saw a friend of my dad's—Tony Pearce. Without knowing it, Tony had been a role model for me while I was growing up. Tony was a successful, semiretired business leader who now spent his time writing books and coaching top executives, and while he looked only a few years older than I, he was light-years ahead in experience and success.

Success had not changed Tony one iota. His warm personality, athletic good looks, and charismatic personality were already legendary in our community.

Before his retirement, Tony was a "turnaround specialist," someone who was able to rescue companies from bankruptcy and lead them to profitability. He had been honored twice by various national organizations as "Entrepreneur of the Year" and was currently serving on a business council to develop a code of integrity for business executives.

During the course of his career, Tony had made millions. He was highly respected in the community because he gave so much of his time and money to help others and because his integrity and ethics were above reproach.

My grandfather would have called him "a real gentleman." My father had the utmost respect for Tony and had often called upon him to serve as a sounding board during his own business career.

Tony was the type of person I aspired to be—wise, respected, confident, and a highly sought-after speaker and mentor. But right now I knew only that I was a long way from becoming the person I wanted to be.

When I graduated from college, Tony wrote me a congratulatory note that—for some unknown reason—I never threw away:

Dear Jeff,

Congratulations on your graduation from college.

You have completed a wonderful period of your life.

Now the learning really begins. I know you will be successful in the field that you choose.

If you ever want to talk about personal or business issues, I would be honored to allow you to learn from my experiences . . . you just have to ask.

Best wishes,

Tony Pearce

Tony had not seen me at the golf course, and it had been a few years since we had talked. I wondered if he would even remember me if I called him. I also wondered if he would take the time to meet with me since he was in such high demand by major corporations all over the country.

After debating whether or not to call him, I finally decided that I had nothing to lose. My life was careening out of control, and something needed to change.

I made the call.

A little nervous as I dialed Tony's number, I was also afraid that he wouldn't remember me and there I'd be . . . feeling like a fool. Even if he did remember me, a few years had gone by and a lot had changed since he sent that note. Maybe his offer was no longer on the table.

When he answered the phone, it took only a few seconds for my nerves to settle down and my fear to disappear. As soon as I said "This is Jeff Walters," he immediately knew who I was. He asked how Mom was doing since Dad passed away, and then he said he was honored that I would call.

I found it interesting that he used the same word— *honored*—he had used in my graduation letter years ago. What a coincidence, I thought after we had finished our conversation.

After some catching up, I reminded Tony of his note from several years earlier. I told him I was having some challenges at work and that I would like his advice . . . if he was still willing to talk with me.

After explaining some of the problems I was encountering, he agreed to work with me only if I was willing to commit to two things:

1. Tony said that he was not interested in helping me solve my problems but he was interested in helping me become a better person and leader, and that would require spending some significant time together. He said that he made it a point to be in town every Monday and if I would commit to meeting with him on each Monday morning for ten weeks, he would be glad to help.

"Ten weeks?" I stammered. "Why ten weeks? That sounds like a long time to me. I don't know if I could be away from work every Monday morning for ten weeks and—"

Tony interrupted. "I use that time span because that will give us a snapshot for most everything that's going to happen to you as you lead your team. It sounds like a big commitment, but I promise, it will go by before you know it."

"If that's what you think and you are willing to commit that much time to me, I will commit that much time to you." I relented. "Sounds like a great opportunity for me."

2. Tony also asked me to commit to teach others the lessons and experiences that he would be sharing with me. He said none of my problems were unique and that others could learn from my experiences.

I was elated when Tony consented to work with me, one on one, for ten weeks. I asked if we could meet on Fridays instead of Mondays, but he said his schedule would not allow that, so I agreed to both of his requirements. After all, I rationalized, if the Monday morning meetings don't go well, I can somehow gracefully bow out of the rest of the sessions.

As it happened, those ten meetings—my "Monday mornings with Tony"—were the best meetings of my life.

The thought that I might "gracefully bow out of the sessions" never again crossed my mind.

As far as my second commitment—to teach others—that is my reason for writing this book.

I am honored you are investing your time in reading *Monday Morning Mentoring* and ask you, in turn, to teach others the wisdom Tony shared with me.

Enjoy the journey, apply what you learn, and continue to grow as you share my Monday mornings with Tony.

The First Monday

Getting Past Splat

It was a rainy, gloomy day when I left home for my first meeting with Tony.

Frankly, I was somewhat cynical about whether meeting with Tony would change anything at work. At best, time with Tony would probably make me feel better about how things were going. I guess I really doubted he could do much to change how I managed. After all, I had worked for years for one of the best companies in the world and had been to numerous management-development sessions. To no one's surprise, however, the impact of these highly touted training sessions rarely lasted more than a short time.

I had to keep reminding myself that if things were great, I never would have called Tony in the first place. The truth was this: I was at a crossroads in my career. Deep down I knew something was going to have to change, one way or another. "Get with it," I chided myself. "Executives all over the country ask for Tony's counsel. You should consider yourself fortunate he has time for you."

We had agreed to meet at eight-thirty. Because of the rain, I drove into Tony's driveway at eight-forty. Tony was waiting for me at the door, looking as if he had just stepped out of *Gentlemen's Quarterly*.

"Hello, Jeff, and welcome!" he said, extending his hand and pulling me toward him for a fatherly hug. "I am honored that you would take your time to come and see me."

Tony asked me to come in and gave me a quick tour. His home was incredible. It was large, with a warm ambiance. His wife had passed away a little over a year earlier, and he was proud to show me several pictures of them taken at locations all over the world. After the tour, he took me to his library, where he said we would be meeting each week.

There must have been more than a thousand books on his library shelves. I noticed several pictures of Tony standing with well-known business leaders whom I immediately recognized. Some of the pictures had been taken in the library where I was sitting. I must admit, I was a little intimidated.

After several minutes of catching up, he said it was time to get down to business.

"Your time is valuable, Jeff," he began, "so I think we need to set some ground rules if we're going to make the best use of our meetings. "With that in mind, I took the liberty of drawing these up while I was thinking about our sessions. See what you think."

He pushed a handwritten note across the table that listed three simple rules:

Ground Rules for
Monday Morning Meetings

Start and finish on time.
Tell the truth.
Try something different.

Simple enough, I thought. I can live with those rules. Then I looked at Tony. "I can handle these. Let's get going."

"Okay then," Tony said. "Tell me what brings you here after all this time."

For the next hour, I did the talking, and Tony listened without saying much.

I began with my college graduation, the last time we had spoken to each other. I had been so excited about the future. Like most grads, I felt nothing could keep me from being successful. I was educated, energetic, and full of optimism.

For the first few years of my career, success came easily and promotions were rapid. I worked in sales for one of the most respected technology-manufacturing companies in the world. Then I was promoted into management—my first big break—and I loved it. Business was good. I went on great trips. I was involved in making some big decisions, and I learned a lot, early on.

My team was not top performing, but our results were acceptable, and more than respectable.

Some of the people on my team didn't have the drive I had, but business was so good, I didn't worry about them.

Actually, I probably ignored performance issues that contributed to the problems I had now.

Oh, and I tried really hard to be "one of the guys." I wanted my team to like me and to want to work for me, so I frequently took them out for dinner and drinks—and even shared some of the issues I was facing. At the time, it seemed like a good strategy. About that same time, I rated the job upper management was doing as far from acceptable. In fact, I even told my team that if we did our jobs like upper management did theirs, our company would go under. We all laughed about that.

Those were the good times. But over the next several years, business got tougher. Most of my team was still intact, but some of the performance issues I had once ignored were now affecting my division's performance in a big way—and by "big," I mean they were becoming threats to my job.

I was working hard—long hours—but business indicators told me things were pretty bad. I wasn't very happy, and the people on my team weren't happy. Our results reflected our frustrations, and the unhappiness transferred over to my home life, as well.

"I looked you up, Tony, so I could learn from you," I said dejectedly. "I'm at my wits' end, and I just hope it's not too late for me to turn this ship around."

After listening for almost an hour, Tony finally started talking. "First," he said, "I know you think these problems and the situation you described exist only on your team. You could not be more wrong. There are few—very few, if any—

leaders who have not faced the same issues you've just shared. I know I have.

"When it comes to leading people, there is no problem that is unique to you. Ask anyone with experience, and you'll discover they've faced the same issues, the same frustrations. So don't feel sorry for yourself. That's a waste of valuable time. Just make plans to make things better.

"Second, it's not too late to change," Tony continued. "You're still young, even though you have a wealth of experience. I admire you for calling me and seeking advice. Few people have the courage to take even that first step.

"Many people facing the challenges you are facing give up too soon . . . just before they turn the corner to success. Successful people keep moving, even when they are discouraged and have made mistakes.

"Jeff, you are in a position almost everyone faces. Every way you turn, it seems you run into a wall."

I nodded. "Exactly . . . and it seems the walls I am running into are getting closer and closer together. I can't seem to get around them."

Tony leaned back in his chair, clasping his hands. "Jeff, you are at a place I call 'splat.' "

"Splat?" I asked. "I have never heard of splat. That must be a consultant acronym describing where I am."

Tony was quick to respond. "No, it is not an acronym or consultant talk. It is a place where most of us visit sometime in our career. Let me explain.

"I once heard a fable about a man who meets a guru on the road. The man asks the guru, 'Which way is success?' The bearded sage doesn't speak, but points to a place in the distance. The man, thrilled by the prospect of quick and easy success, rushes off. Suddenly, there comes a loud 'splat.' Eventually, the man—now tattered and stunned—limps back, assuming he must have taken a wrong turn.

"So he returns to the guru and repeats his question, 'Which way is success?' The guru again points silently in the same direction. The man obediently walks off, and this time the splat sound is deafening. When the man crawls back, he is bloody, broken, and irate. 'I asked you which way to success,' he screams at the guru. 'I followed your direction, and all I got was splatted! No more of this pointing! Talk!'

"Only then does the guru speak, and this is what he says: 'Success is that way. Just a little past splat.'

"Right now you are at splat—tattered, torn, and maybe even broken and irate. But if you are strong enough and dedicated enough to make the effort, we can work together to get you past splat."

"Sounds good to me," I said. "I have been at splat for quite some time, and I am tired of being splatted."

"Obviously, you're facing some real challenges. Seeking an outsider's advice is a good move. We all need people who will help us look at situations from a different perspective," Tony said, his tone riveting my attention. "In fact, I have several people who are my mentors—people who have helped me gain new insights—and who have remained my mentors after all these years. In a nutshell, it's not too late to change, but you will have to work to make improvements.

"One more thing to remember: You're not alone here. Most people have difficulty making the transition from employee to manager and from manager to leader. Your dad once told me something that I will never forget. He said if you want to be extraordinary, the first thing you have to do is stop being ordinary. Wanting to be liked and to be 'just one of the guys' is natural. Of course, everyone likes to be liked. But as a leader, your team should like, or respect, you for the right reasons.

"If your team likes you because you're fair, consistent, empathetic, and a positive person—that's great. But if they like you just because you lavish them with free dinners and drinks, what have you gained? In fact, you're setting yourself up for failure. Why? Because if your goal is to get everyone to like you, you'll find yourself sidestepping tough decisions because you won't want to upset your 'friends.'

"Transitioning from employee to manager or manager to leader requires that you make different decisions, often difficult decisions, and believe me, those transitions can sometimes create challenges in every other area of your life as well.

"I remember when you were a teenager, Jeff. You were so excited when you celebrated your sixteenth birthday and got your driver's license. Remember? You had watched your mom and dad drive for years, and as soon as you were old enough, you went through the driver's education course.

"Now, remember how confident you were? You knew you would be the best driver ever. You even promised your dad with those very words," Tony said with a wink.

"Of course I do," I replied. "I remember even more vividly the second day after getting my license . . . that's when I had my first accident. Thankfully, no one was hurt."

"I remember that, too." Tony nodded. "Most of your soccer team was in the car with you. But, what you don't know is a few days later, your dad and I discussed the main reason for the accident—and that was your failure to understand the difference in responsibilities between being the driver and being a passenger.

"You see, passengers are free to do a lot of things the driver can't do. As a driver, your focus needs to be on the road and not on the distractions. As a driver, you no longer have the right to 'mess around'—like listening to loud music—even though it seems okay to do that as a passenger.

"The same principle applies when you become a leader. You're no longer a passenger. Now, you're the driver. Yet even though your responsibilities increase when you become a manager, you lose some of the rights or freedoms you may have enjoyed when you were a passenger.

"For instance," Tony continued, "if you want to be successful as a leader, you don't have the right to join employee 'pity parties' and talk about upper management. When you're a manager, you lose the right to blame others for a problem in your department. You also no longer have the right to be negative or cynical; you can no longer avoid issues or choose to not make a decision. As manager and leader, the buck stops with you. You are the person responsible for everything that happens in your department, and that's a giant step that is often painful as you make the transition."

But he wasn't through. "You even lose the right to some of your time because you're responsible for other people's time as well as your own," he said, stopping to check his watch. "Speaking of time, what time did you arrive today?"

"A little after eight-thirty," I said innocently.

"And what time did we agree to begin?" Tony wondered aloud.

"Eight-thirty . . . but traffic was heavy and it was raining and I thought I left in plenty of time," I stumbled.

"Yes, it was raining," Tony easily agreed, "but the rain didn't make you late. You see, Jeff, when you accept total responsibility, regardless of what happens or the conditions surrounding what happens, you make adjustments. When it's raining, you leave earlier, or take a different route, or call and change the meeting time. You control if you're on time or not. The rain just forces you to make different decisions."

"I'll remember that," I promised.

"Okay, let's move on," Tony said. "The opposite of accepting responsibility is to find someone or something to blame when there's an issue or a crisis. Of course, there is always someone or something to blame, but a real leader spends his time fixing the problem instead of finding the right person to blame.

"Making excuses rather than accepting responsibility for your actions will destroy your effectiveness as a leader," Tony emphasized. "When you accepted your job, you were not chosen solely to fill a position on the organization chart, you were chosen to fill a responsibility. Nobody needs a leader to find excuses or to find others to blame for failures . . . everyone can do that on their own.

"When you place blame, you focus on the past. When you accept responsibility, you focus on this time forward—on the future . . . and Jeff, until you accept total responsibility—no

matter what—you won't be able to put plans in place to accomplish your goals."

Tony gave me a little time to think that over. It was a
big concept but definitely one I needed to wrap my arms
around.

"One of the first things I want you to understand is
that you have the power to choose to accept responsibility for
improving things," Tony continued. "You have control over
how you react to situations, but I'm going to ask you to eliminate blame from your management style—don't even have
the word in your vocabulary—then you can make some positive changes.

"You see, Jeff, we have control over our choices. I have
found success is ultimately realized by people who make
more right choices . . . and recover quickly from their bad
choices."

He took a sip of coffee before he continued. I was all
ears. "Your choices are directional . . . they lead you toward
or away from the success you are trying to achieve. Day in
and day out, your personal and professional success depends
on repeating good choices . . . and avoiding repeating bad
choices," Tony said.

"Take a look at the successful people you know . . . in
your office, your neighborhood, your city, or your family.
Without exception, their success has been created by their
choices. It's not about luck, the conditions, or even the
guardian angels guiding their lives.

"Now take a closer look at these successful people,
and you'll find they share some common traits, but—

believe it or not—there is not an enormous difference between highly successful people and those who are not so successful.

"For instance, do you think that the salesperson who earns $250,000 a year has five times the intellect or the ability of the salesperson earning $50,000 a year selling the same product in a similar territory?"

"Of course not," I responded.

"So what's the difference?"

"I guess you want me to answer that they made better choices and recovered from their bad choices quicker." I said.

"Right!" Tony answered and then added, "And, another major difference is successful people make choices others don't like to make. If you ask successful people, they may tell you that they may not want to make those choices, either, but they also realize there is often a greater purpose in choosing to do some things they may not want to do.

"When you accept responsibility to make conscious choices for success, you seize the power choices offer and stop being the hapless individual to whom life happens. With good choices, you take control of your success."

Tony glanced at his watch again. "Well, I see we're about out of time today . . . as we agreed." Then he handed me a blue spiral notebook with the words *Monday Mornings with Tony* handwritten across the cover. "Take this notebook and begin writing down what we discuss," he said. "It will be easier for you to keep track when you need to review our discussions."

Tony stood and walked me to the door. "So, is there anything you will do this week to make your situation better?"

"Well, what you said about taking responsibility makes sense, but there are so many external factors working on my team, I'm not so sure I can 'belly up to the total responsibility bar,'" I said sheepishly. "But what I can do, for sure, is not participate in the pity parties and not blame upper management for our problems . . . and I will try to make better choices and take responsibility for everything and see how it goes," I promised.

"Write those things in the notebook when you get home," Tony suggested, "and remember, when you write things down, you commit to doing them. If you simply tell me what you want to do, there is really no commitment to getting it done."

I agreed and told him I would be there at eight-thirty sharp the following Monday.

Driving back to the office that day, I felt even more frustrated. It was going to be pretty hard to accept responsibility for everything happening in my department. I wasn't sure it was realistic . . . and all of the problems I was facing were not the result of my poor choices. I was having a hard time buying his "hapless person to whom life happens" comment.

Some of the things Tony had said made sense, but were his philosophies up-to-date? I wondered. Yet, I had promised. I would try something different and then wait to see what would happen.

Later that day, I opened the notebook to record the

lessons I had learned. Inside the notebook was a letter from Tony that read:

Jeff,

Congratulations for having the courage to seek advice. This step, alone, indicates to me that you have a tremendous amount of pride in your work and, more importantly, that you are willing to take responsibility for your actions. As you turn this page, let the words you write in this notebook become a new blueprint for your success in your business and personal life.

I am honored that you are allowing me to share my experiences with you, and I look forward to seeing you again next Monday.

Best wishes,

Tony

As I read the note, I could feel the genuineness of his words. He sincerely wanted me to be successful . . . and I began to feel more confident than I had in years that change for the good was on the horizon.

Getting Past Splat

*My success depends on having the courage and
tenacity to get past splat.*

I am the driver of my success and happiness!

*Until I accept total responsibility—no matter
what—I will not be able to put plans in place to
accomplish my goals.*

*Transitioning from manager to leader requires
that I make different decisions.*

*My success is the result of making better choices
and recovering quickly from poor choices.*

Keep the Main Thing the Main Thing

I drove into Tony's driveway at eight-twenty. It was raining again, and I waited for a couple of minutes before making a dash toward Tony's house.

He smiled as he opened the door just ahead of my swift trot into his foyer.

"Welcome," he said, "and good job! You made it with time to spare in spite of the weather being much worse than last week. Thanks for coming.

"It also looks like you learned something about responsibility last week since you made some different decisions that allowed you to be here on time today," he added with a smile.

"Yes," I agreed. "I left home earlier, but I'm not sure I did very well with my people, Tony. I tried to accept total responsibility for everything happening in my department, but the rats won the race again this week. Honestly, I have so many things coming at me from so many different directions, it's hard for me to get anything done . . . I mean done well."

"Tell me more," he said, settling into a comfortable wingback chair.

"Well, I have fifteen people reporting to me," I began. "I also have two open positions. Karen, my boss, is demanding—and that's putting it mildly! I'm confident all my people know what they're supposed to be doing, but we seem to get less and less accomplished. We've taken the responsibilities of the open positions and divided them among everyone on the team, but as soon as we put out one fire, another one flares up. I don't have any control over the fires, either. Some of the fires are lit by Karen. Others are created by my team or another department. Regardless of where the fires originate, I'm inhaling smoke all day and finishing nothing that needs to be done."

As I spoke, Tony was obviously becoming agitated and restless. "Are you okay?" I finally asked.

"Well, Jeff, it appears to me that everything is a crisis to you," he said. "So take a deep breath and relax. Your job is not crisis management, and your people should not be firefighters.

"It sounds to me like you think you have no control— over anything—and you've simply become a victim of the circumstances.

"For years I have witnessed people falling into this victim mentality whenever something unexpected happened . . .

something that seemed to be out of their control. They may justify being a victim to themselves and they may think there's a 'grand conspiracy' keeping them from achieving their success. In reality, they are their own worst enemy.

"I've also seen others with an uncanny ability to successfully deal with the unexpected and proactively look for solutions.

"Jeff, there is no 'grand conspiracy' preventing you from accomplishing what you need to do. The unexpected fires are going to continue to blaze, and you have to figure out how to deal with them. Your choice is to be a victim . . . or proactively deal with them and continue moving forward.

"Long-term success," Tony said, "is not an event . . . it is a process that will have peaks and valleys along the way. Falling in the victim trap is in the valley, and remaining in that trap will delay your visit to the peaks."

I knew I was going to sound slightly defensive. "I hear what you're saying, but doesn't everyone occasionally fall into the victim trap? I don't want to be an excuse maker, Tony, but I really don't have control over everything happening around me."

My new mentor was quick to respond, "Of course . . . occasionally feeling like a victim is natural, but remaining in the victim trap will prevent you from accomplishing your goals. So it is up to us to make the choice not to allow ourselves to be victims. It is not easy . . . but it's a choice you make. You control your next move, so will you sit and sulk about all the fires you have to deal with, or will you commit to preventing the fires in the first place?

"That said, I think there are some basic questions that require answers at this point.

The first is, Why do you have two open positions?

Why did these team members leave?

Why do you think everyone on your team knows what they're supposed to be doing if they're not doing it?

What are your priorities?

"Wait. Don't answer those questions now," Tony said. "Just think about them before we meet again next week."

Then, he quickly changed the subject and lightened the mood. "Did you ever see the movie *City Slickers*?"

"It was a great movie . . . an all-time classic. Sometimes I feel like I need to go to that ranch, just to get away. Are you a fan of *City Slickers,* too?" I asked, wondering why he asked me the question.

Tony beamed. "It's a favorite movie of mine . . . probably because I can relate to many scenes in the movie and I remember almost every line. My favorite character was Curly, the hard, crusty old man played by Jack Palance. Curly was full of wisdom, but I think his best advice to Mitch, who was experiencing some of the same midlife questions you are facing, was in one particular scene:

" 'You all come out here about the same age,' he said. 'Same problems. Spend fifty weeks a year getting knots in your rope—then you think two weeks up here will untie them for you. None of you get it. Do you know what the secret of life is?'

"Mitch responded: 'No, what?' "

"Curly holds up his index finger and says, 'This.' "

"Mitch, being a little slow and confused, asked: 'Your finger?' "

"Curly, in his deep voice, responded: 'One thing. Just one thing. You stick to that and everything else don't mean [anything].' "

"Then Mitch asked the million-dollar question: 'That's great, but what's the one thing?' "

"Do you remember Curly's answer?" Tony asked.

After thinking for a second, I said, "I believe that he said something like Mitch had to figure it out."

"Exactly," said Tony. "His exact words were 'That's what you've got to figure out,' and I think Curly's advice of finding one thing and sticking to that one thing would help you get out of your crisis-management mode.

"Now, let me tell you about one of my experiences that happened long before *City Slickers,*" he continued.

"I once worked with a manager who would remind us daily to 'keep the main thing the main thing.' We had banners saying 'Keep the Main Thing the Main Thing.' We had coffee mugs, mouse pads, and notepads reminding us to 'Keep the Main Thing the Main Thing.' It was our mantra— our purpose and priority.

"Every time we saw this person, he would ask us, 'So, what's the main thing?' Everyone knew the main thing and what they did to keep the main thing the main thing . . . and because every person on our team knew the main thing, our corporate and personal vision was laser sharp.

"The responsibilities of leadership can be overwhelming at times," Tony explained. "So many things are coming from so many different directions. That makes it difficult to separate the important from the trivial. So, one of the principle responsibilities of the leader is to keep the main things the main things—the few overriding points or purposes toward which all energy and attentions should be directed at that moment.

"Actually, our main thing was really three things:

> *Equip our team with the tools to be successful.*
> *Provide outstanding service to our customers.*
> *Make a profit.*

"If someone asked us to do something that wasn't part of our main thing, our manager would support us and say we couldn't get it done. We were a focused and productive work group because there was a clear understanding of our purpose."

Then he paused to let that sink in before he continued. "You mentioned that your people know what to do. Why don't you ask them, 'What is the main thing?' They probably have different perceptions of what the main thing is. Some people may think making a profit at all costs is the main thing. Others may think decreasing costs—or just going home on time—is the main thing."

"That's probably the case," I agreed.

"Well, you can't rely on their perceptions, Jeff!" Tony shot back. "I've found when you depend on another's perceptions to match your expectations, you're setting yourself up for disappointment. If you ask everybody what the main this is . . . you may be surprised by your team members' answers.

Tony stopped for another sip of coffee. "We'll spend another Monday on the importance of hiring the right people for your team, but now I think you should try to understand why people chose to leave your team. You probably have some strong opinions, and before I hear them, I want to say it's a natural tendency (but not an accurate perception) to blame pay, benefits, upper management, salary administration, and other factors for someone's resignation.

"But listen carefully because I want this to be very clear: People normally don't leave because of those reasons. People leave because their manager is not meeting their needs. People quit people before they quit companies. They lose trust in the person who is supposed to be leading them, and they start looking for someone else they can trust. I'm not saying that's the case here, but I am saying that in most instances, the boss is the principle reason people resign."

That was painful to hear, but I knew Tony was right on target from my own experiences in resigning from companies . . . but I really did not think that my open positions were because people "quit" me.

"Speaking of bosses, you said Karen is a demanding boss. That's not a bad thing necessarily . . . in fact, being demanding is a good trait. I've heard many bosses called much worse. So how would you describe your relationship with Karen?"

"Well, that's the problem. We really don't have much of a relationship. We have monthly meetings and that's about it. Karen is demanding because she's extremely results focused and is always requesting reports and information. I think she tends to get in our way," I said boldly.

"What are your expectations of Karen?" Tony asked.

"I think she should be a better leader," I began. "She should take the time to meet with me, provide recognition for my team, communicate with me, and help me be better at my job. After all, she's supposed to be my mentor. She doesn't do any of that—she's only interested in reports and results."

"Maybe she should do a better job in those areas," Tony said, "but regardless of how well Karen meets your expectations, you still have fifteen people who are depending on you to develop a positive relationship with her. Therefore, your job is to inform her about what is going on in your department and then achieve results. These are not options. For you to be successful and provide your employees with the necessary tools for success, you and your boss must work together—no matter what."

I was learning quickly that in some matters, Tony allowed no gray areas.

"I can understand why you think it's Karen's responsibility to develop a positive relationship with you," Tony went on, "and you're right. However, if it's not happening, it's up to you to make changes that will make it happen.

"Listen carefully because I had to learn this the hard way. Upward communication goes against organizational gravity and requires courage and persistence on your part.

If you make communication a priority with Karen, your relationship will improve and you will achieve better results."

"That's a lot to think about," I said.

"But, that's just the beginning. Here's the next step: Managing your relationship with your boss involves applying the same principles as leading your team.

"One thing that you control is your attitude and actions toward Karen," Tony explained. "You cannot change her behavior, but you can make adjustments in your attitude toward her and how you treat her. I suggest you take the time and energy to manage your relationship with Karen the same way you manage your team.

"Even though you think she's demanding, she needs you to deliver results. That's her job. I would think she would do whatever she needed to do to help you accomplish your goals. That is how she accomplishes her goals—as long as you are working toward the same goals.

"If she were one of your employees, how would you handle the situation?" Tony asked, ready with an answer to his own question.

"Find out, specifically, what she needs from you and tell her, specifically, what you need from her. For example, do you know what her main things are? Does she know what your main things are? It may be worth setting up a meeting to understand what both of you can do to help each other accomplish your main things. If you asked her, she probably wants to help you work your way out of the situation you are in, but she may not know what you need or what she can do to help. Give her the benefit of the doubt and make your relationship with her a priority. I'll bet she would welcome the conversation."

Tony's case for working on our relationship was a strong one. I was ready to give it a shot.

"Okay, Jeff. Our time is about over for this week's meeting; so what are you going to do differently before next Monday?" Tony asked.

"Clearly, I think you're right about my team not knowing what the main thing is," I admitted. "In fact, I'm not sure I know what the main thing is, myself. So my first job is to figure out what the main thing is and to have a meeting to discuss it with the team.

"I'll also try to meet with Karen to find out what I can do to help her accomplish her main thing. Even though I feel it is not my job, I am committed to work on developing a positive relationship with her—as much as I can.

"And I know we need more focus," I added. "I've let circumstances dictate our actions rather than making room for our mission to dictate our actions.

"I'm also going to try to answer the questions you asked earlier. I have to admit, I really don't think that I have two open positions because of what kind of manager I am, but I'm open to that possibility," I concluded as we walked from the room.

As I left Tony's house, I couldn't get his questions out of my mind: What is the main thing? Why did two people resign? Why do you have all these fire drills?

I had some work to do before our next Monday Morning Meeting.

What Is the Main Thing?

People have different perceptions of what the main thing is.

People quit people before they quit companies.

I have to build a relationship with my boss with the same intensity I maintain in leading my team.

I need more focus on the main things!

Escape from Management Land

G ood morning, Jeff."

Tony met me at the door for our third Monday Morning Meeting, looking as dapper as ever. "Not only are you on time, but you appear to be in a much better mood this week. I hope things are a little better at work."

"Well, I spent a lot of time on the three questions I left here with last week," I confessed. "I think much of my frustration stemmed from not knowing what the problem was—much less what to do to fix it—but I'm pretty sure I've made some real progress this week."

Once Tony had reappeared in the library with two mugs of our now usual coffee, and had settled into his wingback chair, I continued.

"First, I tackled the resignation issue, head-on. I

reviewed Jeni's and Chad's exit interviews. They both resigned during the past couple of months, and, just as I expected, the exit interviews didn't reveal much information. In fact, if you read each of the exit interviews without knowing what they were, you'd think both employees were happy to be working for the company.

"Taking my research a step further, I talked to a few people on my team . . . and while they were reluctant to speak for their former teammates at first, one person—Michael—provided some interesting information.

"Michael said neither Jeni nor Chad really wanted to leave, but they were unhappy about how things had been going in the company. Michael also reminded me both Jeni and Chad received increases in pay shortly before their resignations, so pay had little to do with their decisions to leave.

"Tony, your words from last week kept ringing in my ears: 'People leave because their manager is not meeting their needs. People quit people before they quit companies.' Well, I still felt a specific circumstance—not me or something I did—was the reason they left, but I knew you wouldn't buy that answer, so I went to see both Chad and Jeni.

"I met with each of them, individually, and since they no longer work for me, there was no reason for them to skirt the truth. I'll say up front, both seemed surprised I was interested enough to go see them, and they opened up—more than I expected.

"I was shocked by what I heard. Well, they didn't come right out and say it," I continued, "but I left knowing that they didn't leave the company. They left me—their manager. Just as you said, I wasn't meeting their needs. So during my

visit with each of them, I took a lot of time trying to understand what needs I hadn't met, and, basically, it came down
to three things:

"First, both of them said that I needed to do a better job
hiring good employees. Their perception was I had gotten lazy
in my hiring. In fact, one of them said that if an applicant
could 'fog a mirror,' I would select them for our team. Jeni said
that I 'talked the talk' about how people on the team were important, but when it came to walking the walk, I would dilute
the good people on the team by hiring just about anyone just
to fill a position."

Tony didn't look surprised as I went on. He had probably known what I would hear long before I spoke with my
former employees.

"The problem was my good employees were being
asked to do more and more," I continued, "while others were
being asked to do less and less. Chad even said, 'Some of us
felt abused because we were good employees.' Honestly,
Tony, I couldn't believe what they were saying. Could I be
punishing the good employees by giving them more work
and rewarding the lower-performing employees by allowing
them to do less? Both Chad and Jeni thought so . . . and believed it enough to leave.

"Second, they wanted me to coach every member of the
team to become better. I walked away from both meetings
upset with myself. I hadn't provided adequate feedback and direction to either of these employees, employees I considered
among my best. Really, I assumed—I know what they say
about assuming anything—but I had assumed they were happy
working without much feedback.

"I think I let them down by not paying enough attention to their individual needs," I admitted. "I took them for granted and completely overlooked their desire to learn from me. I didn't think I had much to offer them, but what they really wanted was to be recognized for doing their jobs well.

"One surprise to me was that they wanted to contribute more but I neglected to ask them. That was the main reason that I was so upset with myself. Chad and Jeni were some of the best people I had ever worked with, but I did not use all of their talents—and they were willing and able to do so much more for our team.

"Third, they said they needed me to dehire the people who aren't carrying their share of the load. I think I told you before about performance issues I had ignored. Well, those performance issues had an effect on the rest of the team. Jeni said what began as one negative and cynical employee became a whole team of negative and cynical employees. She said they kept waiting for me to fix the problem, but I allowed it to go on . . . I did nothing.

"Needless to say, Tony, I was humbled after my meetings with Chad and Jeni," I concluded. "I was also a little relieved. At least I now know there are things I can do to avoid losing more good employees."

Tony nodded. "You didn't let me down. That's a good analysis . . . and a good attitude, going forward. So, what about the questions from last week. Find any answers?"

"I combined the last two questions you asked me to address into one: What is the main thing—the main purpose for our team?" I responded, glad that I had completed the assignment before this meeting.

"Wednesday, I had a meeting with my team. I prepared a paper for each team member to complete. On the paper was one sentence: 'The main thing in our department is . . . ,' and each person was asked to fill in the blank.

"Well, I know you won't be surprised by their answers, and really, neither was I. No one knew what the main thing was. Oh, everyone had an answer, but no two answers were the same. Instead of clearly defined goals and expectations, I found mass confusion about our most important mission as a team. This exercise was invaluable!

"Now I know our team has some work to do to define and understand the main thing. But at the same time, it seemed as though everyone felt good about having some direction established."

Tony agreed. "It's like getting in your car and driving in circles. We all need to have a plan and know where we're going.

"So what else did you accomplish during the week?"

"Like you suggested, I had a meeting with Karen . . . and I was surprised at how well it went. I think she appreciated my taking the initiative to meet with her. We still have a way to go, but I'm making it a priority to manage that relationship better.

"And yeah—I am in a better mood this week. I've realized there are things I control that have contributed to my frustrations and the team's frustrations. You know those fires I was complaining about? I found I was doing a good job of supplying the fuel.

"Even though last week was not an ego builder because of some of the answers I discovered, I do feel better. Now I know there is something that can be done, and it's something I can do," I confessed.

"Wonderful!" Tony exclaimed, although without surprise. "You've made some great strides this week, and I'm proud of you. But it sounds like one of the things you discovered is that one of the 'main things' for a leader is to eliminate confusion—which can paralyze your team—because along with confusion comes fear, anxiety, and blurred vision.

"I learned early on that good morale is hard to achieve when people are confused. Creating and maintaining a laser-sharp focus for the team is at the very heart of leadership. And be assured, it's much easier said than done," he explained.

"Today's fast-paced environment demands flexible organizations—ones ready and able to adapt to changing market conditions and technical innovations. But constant changes and the distractions that accompany them can cause us to blur our focus, overcommit, and lock into a knee-jerk, fire-fighting mode . . . not a good place for leaders, or their followers, to be."

I liked Tony's teaching style . . . giving me small "bites" to digest before going on to the larger concepts.

"When you fail to maintain your focus, the team will wander aimlessly in search of direction and clarity, not knowing where to direct their energy and attention. This confusion and complexity creates dissatisfaction and frustration . . . as you've learned.

"The truth is . . . it's usually leaders—not followers—who are responsible for frequent changes in team direction and focus. So beware! If your focus is always changing, expect confusion to be rampant on your team.

My mentor continued, obviously pleased with my report . . . and my attitude. "Something contributing to the confusion on many teams is a trap many managers fall into," he said. "This trap is what I call 'management land,' where things are not always as they seem; there's something else about this place—sometimes it's difficult to escape from management land."

My puzzled expression encouraged Tony's careful explanation.

"There are always 'busy' things to do in management land. If you are not careful, the stacks of paper become the priority. Paperwork rules in management land! People are busy shuffling piles of paper, and when their desk is clear, they think they've been a great leader that day. Also, in management land, simple things often become complex, and people easily lose perspective. Managers begin to think the games others play are what are most important.

"When members of the team enter into management land, people are rewarded for saying only the things managers want to hear. Egos are big, and it's difficult to discover the truth. To the people on the outside, management land can be described as confusing, frustrating, and sometimes comical.

"Many leaders get so engrossed by the management tasks they forget that without a positive, working relationship with their team, they will not accomplish their goals. No matter how brilliant, educated, tenured, or charismatic you are, if you do not escape from management land and stay in touch with your team, you are ultimately going to fail. Every time a leader attempts to make all the decisions and to think that he can stay in management land and 'go at it alone' better than leading a team, something less than the best will happen.

Tony was in his element as he spoke. I jotted notes, trying hard to keep up with his pace.

"What you learned this week is you have to make it a priority to escape from management land and get in touch with your people. Successful leadership requires that you develop a team from whom you can expect honest feedback and earn wholehearted support. Developing your team may not be easy. This requires you to leave the comfort of management land and create consistent feedback from your people.

"You mentioned that Jeni and Chad were disappointed that you did not involve them more in the decisions you made. Most good employees—like those two—want to accept ownership for making things better. But if they do not feel like their input is important to you, they will be remain quiet. It is sort of like owning a car or renting a car. Most people treat rental cars completely differently than they do the cars they own. You may pay as much for the rental car, but you have no ownership. When is the last time you washed a rental car," Tony asked rhetorically. "People respond differently when they have ownership of decisions made on the team."

"There may be some pain involved in escaping from management land. You may have to let go of some things you are comfortable doing. Regardless, it is well worth it. In fact, quality long-term leadership is not possible without escaping management land. Chad and Jeni were right on the mark when they said their expectations of you were simple: Hire good people; coach everyone to become better; dehire the ones who don't pull their share of the load. To do what they

are asking you to do, you have leave management land and
pay attention to your team.

"Jeff, their expectations actually translate into great advice! People want to be on a winning team, which requires
having winners on the team. In a perfect world, every person
on the team would have the desire and talent to be the very
best at their job. But in reality, it seldom happens that everyone is pulling an equal share of the load.

"Let's look at it this way. Most teams are composed of
three performance groups. I call them superstars, middle stars,
and falling stars.

"The superstars are the few people on your team who
have the experience, knowledge, and desire to be the very
best at their jobs. You know who they are, typically 10 to 20
percent of your team—maybe even 30 percent—who do
everything you ask."

I nodded. "I know exactly who they are."

"You probably would like a larger percentage of superstars, but often they are promoted to additional responsibilities, which is the way it should be. Your superstars earned
their way into that category by being consistently outstanding performers. Don't overlook them! In some organizations,
superstars become 'the abused,' as opposed to the 'rewarded,'
because they have to take up the slack for those on the team
who are not carrying their share of the load . . . and that's
not good.

"The second group—normally about half of your
team—consists of middle stars. They may not have the experience to be a superstar yet. Or maybe they are former superstars who, for some reason, lost their motivation to be the

best. They could be your superstars of the future, or they could fall backward.

"Middle stars are your variable performers. Some days they exceed your expectations, and on other days they fall a bit short of what's expected. But here's the irony. As the largest group on your team, the middle stars are the backbone. Your ability to affect the performance of this group is critical to your success.

"Middle stars have their eyes wide open and constantly on you—they watch to see how you treat the superstars, and then they make the decision whether they want to pay the price to be a superstar based on your actions.

"Finally, there are those I call falling stars. Those are the ones who are doing as little as they can get away with. This group is usually quite small, but their impact can be huge! They consistently fail to carry their share of the load. In fact, not only are they not doing their own jobs, but there's also a good chance they're preventing the top performers from doing their jobs as well. This is a group that must be dealt with if you want to be successful.

"A falling star who is not right for the job and who creates a negative environment within the work group will destroy your team," Tony explained. "It is your responsibility to eliminate barriers to your team's success, and if you refuse to address the problem of an incompetent employee, you may need to reevaluate just who is incompetent . . . or who's not doing his or her job.

"If you keep piling more work on your superstars—like Chad and Jeni suggested you did—then you shouldn't expect them to continue to be superstars. Oh, sure, some superstars will always be superstars, regardless of the workload, but others will be beaten down into middle stars because of the additional work you pile on.

"Let's take a look at this chart," he said, pulling a piece of paper from a folder. "Okay, so where is the minimum acceptable level of performance represented on this chart?

> *30% Superstars*
> *50% Middle Stars*
> *20% Falling Stars*

"Of course!" I said. "That's pretty simple. The minimum acceptable performance is in the middle of the 50 percent. Right here."

> *30% Superstars*
> → *50% Middle Stars*
> *20% Falling Stars*

"No, Jeff. The minimum acceptable performance is actually here, at the bottom of the 20 percent," Tony corrected.

> *30% Superstars*
> *50% Middle Stars*
> → *20% Falling Stars*

"You see, the people at the very bottom of the chart are still on your team, so their behavior must be acceptable to you. In fact, many managers—and you probably know some of these people—actually reward their falling stars by giving them less work while acknowledging them with decent performance reviews!

"When you do that, you should expect more people to fall into that category," Tony said. "It's not rocket science that when people figure out they can do less and still get rewarded, they are going to do less. That would be in most people's nature, unfortunately.

"On the flip side, you can probably remember a time when, as a top performer, you were given additional work because your manager was in a time crunch and needed a project completed quickly. I am sure that manager did not intend to 'abuse' you, but in the final analysis, that may have been your perception.

"Abuse your star performers, and you run the risk of their gravitating to mediocrity—which is just the opposite of what you need. Your job is not to lower the bar by adjusting for and accommodating the lowest-performing employees. You should be raising that bar by recognizing and rewarding superstar behaviors!

Again, I nodded in silent agreement.

"You simply cannot hide in management land, ignore performance issues, and expect your superstars to stick around for very long," Tony was emphatic about this point. "That's what Chad and Jeni were telling you. They needed you to coach everyone on the team and to dehire those who didn't carry their share of the load."

"But Tony, it's hard to dehire anybody," I tried to rationalize. "We have so many policies; dehiring takes too long, and I am not sure it's worth the trouble. It's probably a lot tougher now than back when you were involved in a major corporation. You wouldn't believe all the hoops we have to jump through to get rid of a 'falling star.'"

"I never said it would be easy, Jeff," said Tony, ready with a response. "But I did say there's a huge price to pay when you allow people to stay around after they have 'quit.' That is the worst type of employee you can have—one who has mentally quit and is still physically coming to work every day. Even back in my day, it was tough to dehire people. There were stringent rules, just like you have now. Those rules are in place to make sure you are fair and consistent, not to prevent you from letting someone go who has chosen not to live up to your established code of conduct. In fact, Human Resources would be a great help if you have done your job in establishing your code of conduct, providing feedback, and holding them accountable.

"What drives HR crazy is when someone wants to dehire someone who, two months ago, received a great performance review," Tony explained. "I have seen that time and time again—but the manager turns around and blames HR for making it too tough."

"I have seen that happen as well." I said, trying not to let on I have been guilty of that more than once. "But in most cases, I guess I thought I could turn the falling stars around with excellent coaching and not have to let them go."

"Of course there are some you can turn around," Tony agreed, "but you have to make a decision somewhere along the way about how much you are going to invest in the prolonged 'turnaround.' I don't want to discourage you from giving every effort to turn the employee around, but just remember: If you have done everything you can do by establishing the rules, there is a reason for their lack of performance—and in that case even Vince Lombardi could not turn them around.

"There is a price associated with keeping falling stars on the team," my mentor emphasized, "so follow me on this analogy. You know how much I love to play golf, and I think there are hundreds of leadership lessons that can be discovered from the great game of golf."

"Yes, I remember reading one of your first books about golf and leadership. It taught me a lot about both, and I still remember and use some of the tips you shared."

"Great," said Tony, "because this illustration will be in my next golf and leadership book. Not too long ago, I bought a new golf club—a 3-wood—that was going be the answer to my game. It had the latest technology and looked great. The golf magazines gave this club the highest ratings, and I was really proud of my new club until I started hitting balls with it. I hit hundreds of balls on the driving range and on the course. The ball just would not go where I wanted it to go. You can imagine my frustration.

"Finally, after investing $400 in that 3-wood, hours of practice, and many bad shots on the course, I had to make a decision: What was I going to do with this club?

"One of my alternatives was to leave the 3-wood in the bag and try to fool myself into thinking I had not made a mistake. The problem with the 'ignore it' strategy was that I still needed a club to hit the distance of a 3-wood.

"The rules allow me to carry only fourteen clubs, so keeping a club that didn't work for me would prevent me from getting another club that I would trust and could hit consistently. Ignoring the problem was not a good choice.

"Another alternative was to keep using the new 3-wood. Even after hundreds of bad hits, my pride was telling me I was good enough to work it out. I continued using the 3-wood on more rounds and was again rewarded with slices, hooks, rough, trees, sand, and out-of-bounds shots. Hitting this club was driving me crazy, but it was also hurting my game, killing my confidence, and affecting my attitude. Continuing to use the club was not the answer to my problem.

"The alternative I chose was to accept the fact that this club was not right for me. Even though it came highly recommended and had been a great club for other golfers, it was not the right club for my game. Ultimately, I chose to accept the financial loss and the loss of pride, and finally sold that 3-wood to someone more suited for it. My friend who bought it from me (for $50) became a better golfer with the same club that was hurting my attitude, my patience, my ego, and my score.

"Now, I have another 3-wood in my bag I can hit well and feel confident hitting," Tony confessed. "The problem was not my swing or my club. The problem was my swing was not right for that particular club. Once I accepted that I had done everything I could with the expensive, high-tech, good-looking club that did not work for me, I was able to improve my game.

"The same lesson applies to your work. People who are not the best fit for the position on your team may be an exact fit for someone else's position. The faster you act after making a decision to dehire, the better it is for you and your team."

"Great analogy," I agreed. "So let me see if I can nail it down. I can't ignore the falling stars. Give them plenty of time to come around, but after I have done all I can do, I need to move forward."

"Actually, it is their choice." Tony rebutted. "If they know the acceptable code of behavior, the performance expectations, and the consequences for nonperformance, then they have made the choice for you to move forward . . . in a different direction.

"The single greatest 'demotivator' of a team is to have members who are not carrying their load," he continued. "It takes courage to address issues honestly and then let people go when that's necessary. Your emotions are involved, the employee's short-term livelihood is involved, and it is a tough conversation to have. But, if you have provided someone every opportunity for success and yet his performance fails to meet expectations, summon your courage and allow him to go where he can be successful. It is not a personal mistake of yours, nor is it the employee's mistake—the job is just not right for him.

"My experience has been that most of the dehired employees will eventually attest that 'it was the best thing that ever happened to me.' As unbelievable as that may sound, many dehires force people to move from a job that isn't right for them to something more aligned with their talents and interests. With few exceptions, it's also the best thing for the remainder of the team . . . and the leader."

"What you are saying is right on, Tony. Eventually they say the best thing that ever happened in their careers was to be let go." I said. "I can name several people who were let go and then found their 'right job.' But at the time they were dehired, they certainly didn't see it that way. They were bitter, frustrated, and more than angry at management."

"Yep," Tony responded. "That anger and frustration is definitely part of the picture. Trying to save their pride, they blame everyone else.

"Okay, so we've spent a lot of time talking about the falling stars, but you can't ignore your superstars or middle stars, either," he reminded me. "The middle stars are 'on the bubble' contributors. They have the potential to be superstars . . . or falling stars. Your ability to affect the performance of this group is critical to your success.

"Often, it's the 'small things' you do that inspire middle stars to become superstars—things like remembering facts about them and their family, asking their opinions, taking the time to listen or merely doing something special when they need a boost. To raise the performance bar on your team, you have to have your middle stars moving up!

"As far as your superstars," Tony continued, "some managers think that superstars shouldn't be bothered . . . that they want to work independently and deserve to be left alone. That is not normally the case.

"While they may not want or need you telling them what to do and how to do it, they also don't want to be ignored. Superstars are often people with strong personalities and egos who need to know you appreciate their hard work and contributions. If you ignore them, they may think that you don't care about them and may start looking for a place to work where they are appreciated. Pay attention to them!"

Tony paused, obviously thinking before he continued.

"Okay. I want you to try this. Write in your spiral notebook the name of each of your team members and then categorize them as superstars, middle stars, or falling stars . . . and include Jeni and Chad, as well."

"That's pretty easy," I said. "I definitely know my superstars and falling stars. I guess everyone else is a middle star. So I've identified six superstars, including Jeni and Chad. Three team members are falling stars, and eight are middle stars."

"Good," said Tony. "Now, I want you to take that back to your office, go to your files, and retrieve every person's most recent performance review. Then, put their most recent performance review score next to their name. Next, pull their personnel file. Beside each name, note each time that you've documented some kind of recognition or performance improvement over the past six months. It could be a letter of appreciation or a performance improvement document. Please bring that sheet with you next week."

I could see where he was going. It would be a great exercise.

"Well, Jeff, once again, we're out of time, but you're making some great progress, and I appreciate your taking our sessions seriously," Tony said with a smile. "Oh, and by the way, I am enjoying my time with you, as well. So tell me, what are you going to do before we meet next week?"

"Well, I'm going to focus on several things," I began. "First, I will complete the superstars, middle stars, and falling

stars exercise . . . that will be interesting . . . and it's something I need to do. Second, I'll continue my team's discussion on identifying the 'main things' so we can begin
eliminating confusion. Third, I'm going to work with Human Resources to start interviewing to fill the positions that
are open. And finally, I'll begin the process of coaching my
employees. But I am going to need your help in this area because I'm not sure exactly how to do that.

"Tomorrow I'll be receiving the results of my team's
annual corporate survey. I don't think there will be a lot of
surprises in the survey, but it may give us some additional
areas to focus on in our remaining Monday meetings. I'll
share the results with you next week."

"Great! You've got some work to do." Tony beamed,
obviously happy with my change of attitude. "And it sounds
like you've already started thinking about our next meeting. I
will be honored to help you on the coaching part—we will
cover that in one of our sessions."

"See you next week!"

Escape from Management Land

I need to get in touch with my people.

My team needs me to hire good people, coach everyone, and dehire the people who are not carrying their share of the load.

My job is not to lower the bottom by adjusting and accommodating the falling stars. I should be raising the top by recognizing and rewarding superstar behaviors.

I cannot ignore performance issues and expect them to go away.

Tough Learning

I arrived at Tony's house before eight A.M. for our fourth meeting. I had so much that I needed to talk to Tony about and I called him on Friday to ask if we could begin today's session at eight.

"What is it they say about the early bird?" he chuckled, opening the door. "But what brings you here so early, Jeff?"

"I've hardly slept all weekend," I admitted, hoping my words weren't as garbled as I thought they sounded, "and I was hoping we could meet a little longer today . . . because I really need your advice, Tony."

"No problem. Let me get some coffee and we can get started." In minutes, Tony returned with two steaming mugs, settled into his wingback chair, and smiled. "Okay. What's up?"

"When I left last Monday, I was really pumped, but today I feel like I've taken some quantum leaps backward since last week," I confessed. "It all started when I completed the superstar, middle star, and falling star exercise. I've been really inconsistent."

My words were moving faster than my brain, but I wanted to get my story out. "Some of my falling stars actually had better performance reviews than my superstars. I also checked the personnel files, although I already knew what was there—or should I say *wasn't* there."

"And you found . . ." asked Tony, waiting for me to complete his sentence.

"There were no letters of recognition and only one performance improvement documented over the past six months—on a superstar! I couldn't believe it!

"Here's the bottom line: I've lumped everyone into the middle as far as recognition and performance improvement. No wonder Jeni and Chad felt abused! I should have known better. Actually, I did know better, but I did it anyway."

I took a sip of coffee. "Then, our team discussion focused on identifying the main thing, and we did make some progress in that area. Finally, Human Resources is working on finding some candidates to interview as we try to fill those two open positions on my team.

"But now, for the 'new' news. Remember last week when I mentioned I would be receiving the results of our team's annual corporate survey? Every member of the team and Karen, my manager, completed the survey. It's basically their report card on the job I'm doing.

"Frankly, I did not expect any major news to come out of the survey, but when I got the results, I had plenty of surprises. I could not believe what I was reading, but I brought

the survey with me today. Here are some of the 'highlights'
of what my team and boss said:

> Jeff needs to work on being available.
> He needs to make decisions in a more timely manner.
> Jeff needs to improve clarity with direct reports and
> primary accountabilities.
> Jeff rewards mediocrity.
> He spreads himself too thin and does not give
> feedback to anyone.
> Some meetings take two hours to get through one
> hour's worth of material.
> Jeff's biggest challenge is holding people accountable.
> Our meetings are a waste of time.
> He needs to identify and solve problems more quickly.
> He does not hold anyone accountable.
> Jeff needs to be more direct.
> Jeff needs to be more effective at getting issues resolved.

"On a scale of one to seven, with seven being outstanding, the team graded me a four. Can you believe that?" I asked.

"Well, first I should ask if you think the results were
fair and accurate." Tony replied, always the diplomat.

"No, they're not fair," I exploded. "I work my tail off
for these people, and I feel like they betrayed me in an anony-
mous survey. These results go all the way up the organization, and upper management is going to think I'm not doing
my job. I am also more than a little embarrassed."

"I know how you feel. I've had my share of surprises, too," Tony said, trying to salve my wounds. "However, at an emotional time like this, you need to understand things are never as bad as they seem . . . just like in good times, they are never as good as they seem. They are always somewhere in between." Tony added, "My question is, Were there any positives?"

"Not many," I said, pouting, "but here's what they said about my so-called 'strengths':

> Jeff is a good listener.
> Excellent listener.
> He is a team player and hard worker.
> Jeff strives to do the right thing.
> Jeff is committed to win.
> Jeff has a good knowledge of the business.
> He is a great guy.
> He is very personable and effective with the troops.

"There are some great strengths in that list," Tony observed, "but from what you have told me in our meetings, the survey results really should not have come as a surprise. You mentioned in our first meeting that your style was to be one of the guys and have everyone on the team like you . . . you seem to have accomplished that.

"But if you'll remember, I said that if your team likes you for the right reasons, that's a good thing . . . but if they like you only because you bought them drinks and took them out to dinner, it would lead to trouble, which is where we are right now.

"Here's another thing I noticed," Tony continued. "Some of the common responses seem to revolve around the fact that you need to step up to your role as the leader. It sounds to me like your team is begging for accountability."

I nodded, even though I was not convinced that I agreed.

"For sure, it is rare for people to say they want to be held accountable, but in reality, everyone wants everyone else to be held accountable," Tony pointed out. "That's the message they're screaming. They want you to make better use of their time, get out of 'management land' more often, and get in touch with them.

"Bottom line, I don't think they are asking too much. They want you to be their leader . . . not their buddy.

"The papers you have in your hand are valuable! You may not like it," Tony continued, "but those papers contain information most people would pay a lot of money to learn. It reveals the real truth as to how you are perceived as a leader . . . and within that survey you are provided with the information you need to become a better manager. It's a reality check for you, Jeff."

I'm sure I looked puzzled at this point, so Tony offered some clarification.

"The survey is a reality check. Because the pace of business is faster than ever these days, most people don't stop long enough to take a reality check, so they keep doing the same things until they run out of options.

"It's also important to realize you're not the first person

to be shocked into reality by a survey. Sometimes we are in such a hurry with our demanding schedules, we don't take time to stop to refill our professional fuel tank—until we are on the freeway at six in the evening, praying we can make it to a gas station before our vehicle sputters to a stop. It seems like this survey came along just in time."

"Just in time?" I wondered out loud.

"Because you still have options available," Tony pointed out, "and it is not too late to do things differently.

"Now, if you're willing to listen to their comments and learn from them, let's spend this session talking about it. If you are going to be defensive and try to justify your position on every remark, our time would be best served doing something else. It is your choice."

"It will be tough for me not to give my side of the story and justify why things are the way they are," I countered. "I'm disappointed and hurt, but the reason I came to you in the first place was to get myself out of the ditch I'm in, and maybe this information will help me do that."

"Great. Then let's dig deeper into this survey to see what your team wants from you.

"In a perfect world," Tony began, "we want everyone to agree with our ideas, and we want our actions to be praised as the best ever. But the reality is that we will have critics . . . and having critics is a good thing. Our choice comes when we decide what we do with the criticism that comes our way.

"You probably don't want to hear this, but in my book, you're wasting your time, reacting to every critical comment on the survey," my mentor pointed out. "Some of those comments are personal—the person who wrote them may not like you for whatever reason.

"That type of criticism—criticism focused on your person—will never help you become more successful as a manager. In fact, those critics are not worth spending your time on, trying to understand. Instead, focus on the critical comments that can help you learn from your mistakes so you can achieve your goals. The people making personal criticisms, even though these folks may be vocal, could be alone in their thinking.

"Personal critics remind me of a story about an old farmer who advertised his 'frog farm' for sale. The farm, he claimed, had a pond filled to the brim with fine bullfrogs.

"When a prospective buyer appeared, the old farmer asked him to return that evening so he might hear the frogs in full voice. When the buyer returned, he was favorably consumed with the symphony of magical melodies emanating from the pond, and he signed the bill of sale on the spot.

"A few weeks later, the new owner decided to drain the pond so that he could catch and market the plentiful supply of frogs, but to his amazement, when the water was drained from the pond, he found that all the noise had been made by one old bullfrog.

"The same may also be said about people who criticize your person. Don't allow the critical noise of 'one old bullfrog' keep you from doing what you need to do."

Tony chuckled before he continued. "Okay, now let's focus on the criticism that is of value to you. In the survey, there are some common concerns we should embrace—and you need to accept these concerns as the truth. . . . It is what it is.

"Ultimately, we all need criticism, no matter how successful we become. Criticism whips our fragmented attention into a laser focus on some of the more important aspects of our jobs and our lives. I believe criticism is a 'teaching tool,'" Tony said. "More specifically, it is a learning tool that teaches us hard lessons throughout our lives.

"Unlike the way that many people think, I strongly feel that criticism isn't always negative. In fact, in many forums, such as your employee survey, criticism is a positive, necessary part of growth.

"The healthy approach to criticism is to pay attention to it," Tony emphasized. "Always listen with the intent to understand why the criticism is being leveled at you and why the critic may want you to know his or her feelings.

"And there's an upside to criticism, too. Criticism from the right people could lead to improvement. Many employees dread performance reviews or employee surveys. They know that criticism is on the way, even though there are probably more positives than negatives in performance reviews. The people who pay attention to the feedback and make adjustments based on that feedback are the ones who will ultimately get the next promotion."

I nodded my agreement. That had been my own experience.

Tony continued. "The biggest room we have is the room for improvement. There's always something we can do better, do more often, or do with a different intensity. Appropriate criticism helps us focus our attention on what we need to do to become more successful.

"All my life, I have heard people boast, 'I welcome

constructive criticism,' but sometimes that invitation is hard to believe. Why? Because of our human nature, constructive criticism carries a certain sting, even though it may help us correct a wrong, strengthen a weakness, or chart a more successful course.

"One reason for criticism's stinging effect is something referred to as 'psychosclerosis,' which comes from the Greek term *psyche,* or 'mind,' and the Latin term *sclerosis,* as in 'hardening of.' I call it hardening of one's imagination. Our natural tendency is to think our idea is the best—or the only—idea that will work. The second phase of full-blown psychosclerosis is becoming closed-minded to any suggestion. So if we think we have the best or only idea and we're closed to any suggestions, the result is that we become stagnated in our own stubbornness.

"I don't think I've ever heard that term," I said as I wrote the definition on my notepad.

"It's not a frequently used or well-understood concept," Tony explained, "and the opposite of psychosclerosis is the ability to be flexible—listening with the intent to learn so that you can make a better-informed decision.

"So once you make the choice to accept criticism as a learning tool, here are a few suggestions:

1. Acknowledge that criticism is a form of feedback—and we all need feedback.
2. Ask yourself these questions: Who's offering the criticism? Is he or she qualified? Is he or she trying to hurt you, personally, or trying to help?

Objectively, is there any truth to what this
individual is saying?

3. Constructive criticism is a gift. Thank the giver.

4. Be willing to learn from what's been said. Don't
    put your self-esteem at the mercy of others.
    Liking who you are makes it easier to evaluate the
    criticism of others.

5. After you have a chance to review the criticism,
    communicate clearly how you feel and think about
    the criticism. Then take appropriate action to
    improve.

6. If you want constructive criticism from others
    (and you should), be willing to return the favor if
    they are interested.

"Those are great points," I said as I scribbled them down.

"Bottom line, criticism is a fact of life," Tony continued. "You have the choice to perceive criticism as a hin-
drance or a help. Experts in human behavior encourage us
to be prepared to accept criticism and to accept it gra-
ciously.

"Realistically, criticism—both constructive criticism
and criticism that is less so—should become a tool with
which we grow as individuals while evolving our skills and
our ideas. Ultimately, we can find the comfort zone—the
fine line between dismissing criticism and clinging to each
word we hear—and we also can learn to welcome criticism
rather than become defensive when criticism comes our way.

"This survey should be the beginning of a process to

start making improvements," Tony pointed out, "and I would
suggest you do three things as fast as you can:

1. Have a meeting with your team and review the results
of the survey. Acknowledge that the information they
provided you is valuable and that your intent is to
understand it better so you can make some
leadership adjustments.
2. Ask for their feedback. What do they suggest that you
can do to improve. Listen with an open mind. The
information you receive back is valuable!
3. Create an action plan to improve. Share it with
your team and your boss and ask them to hold
you accountable.

"So, what do you think?" Tony wanted to know.

I took a few moments to try to understand what I really
thought before putting it into words. "I know I don't like to
be criticized," I began, "but there is a good chance this criticism is a blessing in disguise. After listening to you, maybe
what my team has given me is a gift that I need to accept. I
am not happy with it—I wish they had come to me, face-to-
face, with their feelings—but I know I would have been defensive about it, and then nothing would have changed.

"This week I am going to conduct the meeting you suggested. I will thank my team for their candor, ask for feedback, and begin an action plan to improve," I decided. "Like
I told you before, I'm in a leadership ditch—I just didn't

know how deep the ditch was—and I'm going to do what I can to work my way out. Our meetings and this survey give me the shovel I need to start digging my way out of it."

"Great, Jeff. You didn't let me down—and I know this type of information is tough learning." Tony smiled. "Good luck next week in your meeting. I will be eager to hear all about it."

Tough Learning

Understand that everyone needs to be held accountable, including me.

Focus on the criticism that is constructive and not personal.

Accept constructive criticism as a gift.

Acknowledge that criticism is a learning tool that teaches us lessons throughout our lives.

The "Do Right" Rule

As I arrived at the Tony's house, I could see him through the window, talking on the phone. As soon as he hung up, he hurried to the door and greeted me—on time—with his patented handshake and man hug. I could tell the phone call was something special because he was beaming.

Before I could say a word, Tony was ready to fill me in: "Jeff, I just hung up the phone from my son Huntleigh. He is now living in Houston, and he just called to tell me he and Kim are going to make me a grandfather this fall. I've been looking forward to this day for a long time."

He paused, seeming to savor the moment, and then announced, "I certainly don't feel old enough to be a grandfather, but I am just thrilled. What a day!"

I had never seen this side of Tony. We had always been in "deep" serious discussions during our meetings, and here I was looking at a proud man who had just learned he was going to be a granddad . . . and I was the very first to hear it from him. "That is fantastic news. Congratulations! I can tell you are pumped. Do you want to postpone our meeting so you can begin sharing the news with your family and friends?"

"No, the news can wait an hour or so while we focus on our meeting. But I must admit, I'm looking forward to telling my golf partners this afternoon. I am the last one in my group to have the honor of being a grandparent, and I'll have ample time to brag this afternoon."

After getting our coffee, we settled into our usual places in Tony's comfortable library.

"Well, let's get down to work," he said. "I've been looking forward to hearing what happened with your survey results meeting. So, how did it go?"

"I think the meeting went pretty well," I began. "I was able to listen to their concerns and come up with a plan to address some of the areas the team mentioned. They also seemed to appreciate having the opportunity to express themselves. It was obvious I had not done a very good job of listening to them in the past . . . and they seemed surprised I cared.

"The things you said about management land were exactly right. I was spending far too much time in management land and not enough time with my people," I said. "Fortunately, that is something I can fix if I focus on it. Needless to say, I was pleased with the response from my team.

"The meeting was last Tuesday, and that was the highlight of my week. The remainder of the week was tough, and I really need your advice and counsel on a problem that reared its ugly head Wednesday. I'll be honest. I have not been able to sleep very well since then because this problem is big, and it has some huge ramifications for my team and me.

Tony leaned forward, signaling that I had his full attention.

"A few weeks ago, an area that I committed to start working on was coaching my team. I knew that I had not been doing a great job in that area and that I would need your help. But I assumed coaching the superstars and middle stars would be fairly easy. I mean, all I thought I needed to do was provide them with positive recognition, get out of their way, and let them do their job. I guess I thought falling stars represented the only areas where I would need to address tough performance issues.

"However, I have a major issue on my team, and it involves one of my superstars, who also exerts a lot of influence on the other team members. Here's the deal: Todd has been with our company for six years. He's really good at his job and has a good relationship with all his teammates. He is dependable, consistent, and knowledgeable. I think he is one of my very best employees.

"Not too long ago, he would volunteer for any special project I needed," I explained, "but he hasn't been volunteering much recently. I just thought he was taking a break from additional responsibilities and allowing others to do some of the extra things.

But three weeks ago I discovered that Todd has been drinking on the job. I talked to him about it, and he said he understood it was wrong, but he was working through some personal issues and was just trying to cope as best he could.

"I told him I understood, but drinking during work hours is against our company policy and our team's code of behavior. So, after consulting with Human Resources, I wrote him a warning letter, stating that the next violation would lead to termination. He acknowledged the problem, signed the letter, and said that it would never happen again. I really believed him.

"Well, last Wednesday I saw Todd drinking again. I happened to be walking by his office around two o'clock, and I saw him pouring some scotch into his coffee mug. I don't think he even saw me, and I just kept walking down the hall.

"No one else knows about this situation," I confided. "If HR knew, they would have already asked me to terminate him. To my knowledge, no one on the team knows about his problem. At the same time, I feel for him—I know he's struggling, and I really want to help him.

"Also, I remembered what you said about raising the bar, not lowering it. If I let him go, then I would have *three* open positions and I would have lost another one of my superstars, which doesn't help my situation.

"What I think I want to do is to 'forget' what I saw Friday and just watch to see if he does it again. What do you think?"

Tony was sympathetic. "I understand where you're coming from, Jeff. I've been there, too. These types of decisions are gut-wrenching, and, no, I'm not going to tell you what to do. This must be your decision. However, I am going to ask you some questions that may help with your decision-making process.

"First, does Todd understand the company policy and your team's code of behavior about drinking on the job?"

"Yes." I nodded. "In fact, we discussed it in detail in our performance counseling three weeks ago and he had to sign a document stating he clearly understood the policy as well as the potential consequences."

"Are the policy and your expectations reasonable and fair?" Tony asked.

"Yes, I believe they are," I answered.

"What would you do if one of your falling stars was caught drinking on the job?"

"That's easy," I said. "I would dehire him and move forward. But this isn't so easy. Todd is having personal problems, and he's one of my few superstars . . . and besides, I'd be lowering the bar, not raising it! I also feel obligated to be as fair as I can to him. He has been a loyal employee for a long time."

Tony paused before his next question. "So what is the right thing to do?"

"I really don't know," I responded. "I want to be empathetic and help him, but I know he broke the rules. The right thing to do, probably, is let him go. But I would be the one paying the price to do the right thing because then I would have another open position and one less superstar. Frankly, that doesn't appeal to me."

"Okay, Jeff. Let's think about this from a couple of different perspectives," Tony directed. "First, you've mentioned several times that you would be lowering the bar if you let

Todd go. I don't agree with you. It sounds to me as though you're using that statement to justify not doing the right thing.

"And before you say anything, let me explain. You have two competing emotions—one being what is right, and one being what is easy. It is tough to make a good decision when those emotions are competing against each other.

"Your job is to raise the bar for long-term, sustained success, not for short-term convenience. Short-term results are easy. You can threaten people, pay them more, or just give them what they want, and you'll get short-term results.

"Achieving long-term results is much more difficult," Tony pointed out. "It requires establishing a code of behavior that must be followed. It requires providing accurate feedback. It requires delivering the consequences—positive and negative—based on decisions that employees make. It requires that you hold people accountable—one of the areas of improvement identified on the survey. All of these require courage—your courage—to do the right thing.

"People can be superstars in one area and falling stars in another area. You've categorized Todd as a superstar based on your performance criteria," Tony continued. "However, it's obvious that he's a falling star based on your code of behavior, so you need to address this issue as though he's a falling star because that's what he is at this point in time.

"Second, I subscribe to the 'Do Right' Rule. Simply stated, do what is right even when no one is watching! Of course, doing the right thing isn't always easy. In fact, sometimes it's really tough, but just remember that doing the right thing is always right.

Tony gave me time to let that last sentence sink in. Then he continued.

"Now if you don't have a code of behavior or performance expectations, it's difficult to know what is right. In this case, that's not a problem . . . at least it doesn't appear to be a problem, based on what you've said. You said he understood the expectations and even signed a document stating that if he continued to drink on the job, he could be terminated.

"I'll be the first to acknowledge that sometimes it's difficult to know what is 'right' when you are mired in a crisis like the one you are facing with this situation. But you're in the middle of a real-life, personal 'integrity check.'

"Your situation is similar to when you install new software on your computer. Once loaded, it will automatically run what is called an 'integrity check,' a series of tests to determine if any part of the program has been lost or damaged. If any piece of the code in that program doesn't have complete integrity, the program as a whole can't be trusted. At best, you would have a program that wasn't functioning properly. At worst, using a program lacking integrity could cause you to lose valuable data or even damage your computer, so the integrity check is vital.

"This situation—Todd and his drinking on the job—is *your* personal integrity check. You know what is the right thing to do, but your emotions are guiding you to follow the path of least resistance. In this case, the path of least resistance is to ignore what you saw and hope nothing more will happen. That is probably not realistic and will lead to other problems down the road. But while you are in the middle of the crisis, it is easy to justify ignoring the problem.

"Choose your path carefully," Tony admonished. "Sometimes the decisions that seem so minor become major over time. That's also how your personal integrity is lost—one degree of dishonesty at a time—and many times you are not even aware of the severity of the situation.

"My own experience has taught that the best decisions are normally made before you're in a crisis," Tony went on. "You can think more clearly and evaluate alternatives better before things go haywire.

"I learned that from a friend of mine who is a pilot. He once told me that every conceivable problem that could happen while he was flying the plane had been simulated, documented, and placed in a contingency manual in the cockpit. That manual documents everything that can go wrong and what actions to take if there's a problem.

"You see, pilots don't make decisions when they're in a crisis—they implement plans that were made before the crisis. For example, if a light flashes signaling a hydraulic problem on the aircraft, the pilot opens the manual and finds the procedure for correcting the problem. Then he implements that procedure.

"It would be difficult for a pilot to think of everything he might need to do while he's in a crisis and the plane is losing altitude," he pointed out.

"In business, from time to time, we see lights flashing, indicating we have a problem. When that happens, some managers will throw a rug over the light so they can't see it flashing.

In other words, they ignore it. Sure, they may feel better, but the company is still losing altitude.

"Other managers may unscrew the bulb . . . no more annoying flashing light. They may even pass the bulb to another department. But when they check the other business gauges, the company is still losing altitude.

"Some may smash the light with a hammer. That makes them feel better temporarily, but the company is still going down.

"The only way to fix the problem is to go directly to what's causing the light to flash and fix the cause. Like the pilot, an action plan should have been decided upon long before the crisis developed.

"If you think about it, you're in the middle of a crisis right now—lights are flashing—and your vision is cloudy. Sure, it's easy to justify going down the least painful path and ignoring the problem instead of doing what is right. But the truth is the problem won't just go away. You have to take action. You have to do what is right and resolve the issue.

"I read where Confucius once said, 'To know what is right and not do it is the worst cowardice.' It sounds as though even Confucius subscribed to the 'Do Right' Rule. But actually living the 'Do Right' Rule is tough because it requires discipline, commitment, and courage. Think about it. . . ."

There was another pause. What Tony was teaching made sense.

"My third question, Jeff, is, Why do you think you're the only one seeing the problem? Many times the manager is the last to know about a problem on the team," he said. "What the manager sees is normally a very small part of the whole. It's like an iceberg in the ocean. Above the water you can see the tip, but what lies below is much larger, much more powerful, and, usually, much more destructive.

"The closer you are to the situation, the more you can see. Todd's teammates are closer to this 'iceberg' than you are, and I would be surprised if they're not wondering why you are allowing Todd to do what he's doing.

"Fourth, *everything* counts when it comes to your leadership. If you think ignoring the problem doesn't matter, you're wrong. You're always leading, even when you're ignoring a problem and thinking no one else is looking. Your team doesn't really care if your company has an ethics department or compliance officer. What matters to your team is what you do . . . and everything you do matters because your team is watching . . . and depending on you to do the right thing.

"One thing about the 'Do Right' Rule. There are two sides to doing what is right. Once you discover what the right thing to do is, you either do it or you don't. There is a huge gap between what is right and what is wrong . . . and there is no gray area. You cannot straddle the integrity gap. You are either on one side or the other—and you have to be consistent.

"Some people would like to think that what they do really doesn't matter," Tony continued, "and what difference does it really make if you sacrifice your personal values for values that are accepted by many as normal? Well, it makes a *big* difference, because people are watching us, and everything we do makes a statement about which side of the integrity gap we stand on. Doing what is right protects you from the slippery slope of telling one small lie that leads to another lie . . . and another.

"Ignoring the problem is not a good solution, either. Ignoring issues puts your own integrity at risk. If you lose your integrity, you won't be able to develop or maintain trust, the very basis for every relationship. Jeff, I can't say this enough: You must guard your integrity as if it's your most precious leadership possession because that really is what it is. But you are the leader here, and the choice is yours.

"Obviously you have a decision to make. So what are you going to do?"

Tony's message was clear but difficult at the same time. "Okay, I know everything you said is probably correct," I began, "but it's hard to do what is right when the pressure is on. I'm not looking forward to three open positions, one less superstar—at least in most areas—and facing Todd, knowing he's going through some personal issues. It's tough. Plus, I really think that this problem is isolated to Todd—I don't think it impacts the rest of the team.

"But, I know I've been fair . . . and I know he made the choice to put his employment at risk. Maybe you're right, I may not be the only person aware of the issue. There is a chance that others on the team are watching me and judging me on how I handle this situation."

As I went over the points Tony had made, the big picture began coming into focus.

"Okay. This is my plan. I'm going to Human Resources as soon as I get back to the office, and I'll get their help in working my way though this issue."

I took another deep breath. "Well, Tony. It probably won't surprise you that I already see a place where I need some help from you next week. You mentioned we would discuss hiring at one of these sessions . . . I think I need to do that pretty fast. Can we do it next week? I'm going to have to make some good hiring decisions—especially now. Wish me luck."

"Good luck, Jeff," he said as we stood in his library, "and we'll plan to cover hiring next week. In the meantime, you are going to be fine as you work through this issue. Look at it this way. It's a temporary problem—a temporary problem you have to face. Remember, too, that leaders who have integrity possess one of the most respected virtues in all of life. If you can be trusted to do what is right, whether alone or in a crowd, and if you are truly a person of your word and convictions, you are fast becoming a unique and valued leader.

"People respect others whose audio is in sync with their video. In other words, those who are consistent in doing what they say they will do. When you discover what the right thing is, then it is up to you to have the courage to do it.

"I look forward to next week and to hearing about how you handled this challenge. Keep your chin up . . . you will do fine."

"Thanks, Tony. Enjoy your day sharing your great news! Huntleigh is very fortunate to have you as his dad . . . you are a special person," I said, walking down the front steps and heading out to my car.

"Thanks for your encouragement. This will be an interesting week. See you next Monday," Tony called with a wave.

Do the Right Thing

I have to acknowledge that doing the right thing is always right.

I need to develop my integrity check action plan before I get into a crisis.

I need to remember that problems don't just go away.

I have to guard my integrity like it's my most precious management possession.

The Sixth Monday

Hire Tough

As I drove up to Tony's house, I could see him at the door. "Hey, Jeff," he called, "this week I'm the one who could hardly wait for our meeting. In fact, I was tempted to call you several times to find out how your week was going, but I held myself back. So fill me in."

We got our coffee and sat down in the wingback chairs. "First, how was your week, telling all of your friends about your big news?" I asked.

"It was terrific. I'm still on cloud nine and already envisioning the excitement of being a grandfather. I never knew I would be so excited about this stage of my life, but here I am, and I'm ecstatic. But tell me, how did your week go?"

"Well, it was an interesting week, to say the least," I began. "I left here and went straight to Lynn in human resources to discuss the Todd issue. She asked me some of the same questions you did, and we decided I didn't have a choice.

I had to terminate Todd for drinking on the job. She suggested three things that really helped me through this tough time: She said we needed to 'role-play' the termination and think through every reaction Todd could conceivably have. She also said to go to a 'neutral' site—I picked the conference room. And she said that we needed to have all of his paperwork ready. We were not walking into a debate; we were there to implement a decision that he had made.

"So Lynn and I began role-playing the discussion I was about to have with Todd. Tony, I was very uneasy about the whole situation, but the role-play helped me feel more prepared and confident. I also asked Lynn to witness the termination session. We computed his final pay, got payroll to cut the check, and called him into the conference room.

"Lynn's advice to me before the session was to do everything we could to maintain Todd's self-respect and dignity while being firm and fair with him.

"When Todd walked into the room, he obviously knew something was up. I asked him to sit down and began talking to him about the drinking problem. He was stunned I would terminate him for something 'as minor as this.' He also accused me of not having any compassion because he was going through some personal problems.

"Obviously angry and frustrated, Todd then went on to say the team wouldn't survive without him because he was more the leader of the team than I was.

"Thankfully, Lynn and I had anticipated and role-played all of his reactions. She had told me that the majority of people who are fired feel the same way: It's always someone else's fault, management has no heart, and there are extenuating circumstances.

"I must admit, she did a great job in preparing me for the meeting. Her last piece of advice before we began the meeting was to remember that Todd chose to fire himself. We were only implementing the decision that he made himself. That thought made me feel a little better.

"Anyway, the meeting was thirty extremely long minutes of intense emotions. I really felt badly for Todd, but I kept remembering that I was only implementing *his* decision. Finally, he understood we weren't going to change the decision that he had made, so he took his check, cleared out his desk, and left.

"After taking a few minutes to steady my own emotions, it was then time for my weekly team meeting. Of course, the first thing everyone wanted to know was what happened to Todd. He had left without saying anything, but they saw him cleaning out his desk.

"I told them that Todd was no longer with our company and that my number-one priority was to fill his position as soon as possible. They asked what happened, and I followed Lynn's advice, again, saying I would not go into any details other than that we have to work together to take up the slack we all feel without Todd. I promised them that I would find the right person to fill his job.

"Here was my surprise. I overheard Kevin and Shannon, two of my middle stars, saying they were relieved they wouldn't have to cover up for Todd's drinking any longer.

I don't know if I was the last to discover his drinking on the job, but I do know I wasn't the only person aware of the problem. My team was watching, and my integrity was being challenged. Tony, you were right again.

"The rest of the meeting went well. We finalized what the main things were for us to accomplish, and here are the three main things we came up with:

1. Treat each person on our team with dignity and respect.
2. Deliver outstanding service to our customers.
3. Provide profits to our company.

"Sound familiar? Almost the same as the main things you told me several weeks ago. I told the team they will be asked, every day, what the main things are, and I also told them if what they were asked to do by someone else didn't fall into these three areas, they had the right to say no—regardless of who asked.

"So, all in all, the week was not too bad. Losing Todd created some logistical issues, but we worked our way through them. I also learned I should have involved Lynn in Human Resources long before I did. She knows her stuff and wants to help me.

"In the meantime, she has identified twenty candidates for me to interview for my three open positions, and I have interviews scheduled on Wednesday, Thursday, and Friday of this week. My plan is to fill these positions by the weekend, so I'm eager to hear what you have to say about hiring."

Now it was Tony's turn to talk. "Well, I'm glad everything worked out with the Todd situation. Jeff, you did the right thing, even though it was tough. I'm proud of you.

"With respect to the hiring, let's start with a question: What is the most valuable asset in your company?"

"That's easy," I said. "People are the most important resource in any company. People make the company . . . any company."

"Okay. Now tell me, what is the greatest liability of your company?"

This question was more difficult. "Hmm. I would think that something like product failure would be our greatest liability."

"Well, I don't agree with you on either point," Tony responded.

I couldn't hide my surprise . . . and my confusion. "I'm not sure I'm right about the greatest liability," I defended, "but I know I'm right about people being the most important asset in our company. How could you argue that? Customers judge our company on the people they deal with. So people are the most important asset."

"I agree with everything you said, but my question was a trick question," Tony admitted. "The most important asset in your company is having the *right people* on your team. If you have the right people on your team, you have a great chance to be successful.

"The greatest liability in your company could be having the *wrong people* on your team. In fact, there is nothing any competitor can do to hurt your team as much as having the wrong person on your team," he explained.

"The most important thing you do as a leader is to hire the right people. You cannot have a strong and effective team with weak and ineffective people.

"Jeff, you have a great opportunity right now. With three open positions, you can make a big difference in the makeup of your team. You can add some diversity, generate new ideas, and add some energy and spark by picking the right people.

"You said you wanted to hire these three people by the weekend," he continued. "I don't think that is reasonable. Your job is to hire tough and not just pick the first person who meets the minimum qualifications. You need to make it a privilege for someone to earn his or her way on your team. If you hire tough, it will be a whole lot easier to manage the *right people*.

"The decision you have to make is to hire tough and manage easier, or hire easy and manage tougher. I can assure you, the best thing to do is to take your time on the front end so that you can enjoy having the *right people* on your team.

"When you begin the process of interviewing and hiring," Tony explained, "understand up front that you are probably not a great interviewer. Don't take that personally. It's not a poor reflection on you. How many people have you hired in the past couple of years?"

It did not take me long to come up with my answer, "I hired two people last year and one the year before. I have not had a lot of turnover until recently."

"Jeff, if you are hiring only three people in two years, you are not going to be a great interviewer unless you have a great interview system. It is not that you can't be a good interviewer, it's just that you don't use your interviewing skills very often. Not many managers do. If you don't use the skills very often, you need a good system to help you make the best decision.

"I'm sure Lynn in HR will provide you with an interviewing track to follow, and you may even want to ask her to participate in the hiring process with you," Tony suggested as he stopped to take another sip of coffee.

"Okay. Here are some pointers that will help you make better decisions.

"The first mistake many people make in interviewing is lack of preparation—they make it a subjective decision based on personality rather than an objective decision based on fact. To hire tough, you have to prepare tough. Many people begin preparing when the candidate is in the lobby. How can you make a great decision if you are not adequately prepared for what you want to decide upon? Your preparation should begin long before the candidate is in the lobby. In my book, lack of preparation is no way to treat someone who may become your most valuable asset. Instead, prepare every question—and your ideal answer—in advance so you spend your time listening and evaluating instead of trying to figure out what question you want to ask next.

"Another problem generally associated with interviewing is that you're always emotionally involved. The open position is taking time and energy away from you, so you want to fill the job fast. Your emotions want the person to 'fit' even though he or she may not be the right fit. Fight those emotions. You will be far better off by taking your time and getting the right person," Tony said. "I suggest you ask Kim or someone in HR to help—they're not faced with the same emotions you have about these openings.

"In hiring I recommend the Three Rules of Three, which I think you should follow to prevent your emotions from making a hiring decision for you:

> Interview at least three qualified candidates for
> every position.
> Interview the candidates three times.
> Have three people evaluate the candidates.

"I know that sounds like a long process, but remember— your job is to hire tough."

I was scribbling notes as fast as I could. These were excellent guidelines . . . and I planned to use them.

"Lynn has already provided you with twenty qualified candidates for the three positions," my mentor pointed out. "That's good. You have more choices. After the initial interviews, narrow the field down to your best nine candidates. I would schedule second interviews with those nine candidates at times that are different than their original interview times. In other words, if your initial interview was in the morning with one person, interview that person the next time in the afternoon or evening. You'll be working with these individuals all day, so why not see what they're like at different times?

"Since you and Lynn are involved in the process, you may want to invite one of your superstars also to be involved. The superstar may be able to give you some insight on how the candidate would fit with your current team. Many superstars look upon this type of involvement as a reward. You will also find that your superstar will take an immediate ownership into the person you wind up hiring and help in his or her orientation. That is a good deal for everyone. As a word of caution, if this helping in the interview process is not something that the superstar enjoys, don't force him to do it. But, if he's interested in helping, he can be a great source of information.

"Don't 'stretch' the candidates into being what you want when they are not. If there is any question whether a person is qualified or not, pass on that one and keep searching for the right person," said Tony. "I have seen many 'on the border' candidates hired and later the manager discovers that she may have stretched her evaluations a bit to consider them 'on the border.'

"Never forget this: What you see candidates exhibit in the interview will not get significantly better once they are hired. Oh, they will have more experience but their smiles will not be brighter, their attitudes will not be better, their personal hygiene will not be better, and their willingness to do whatever it is you would like will not be at the same level when they are on the team. You are seeing them at an interview—where they are putting their very best foot forward. The bottom line is what you see will not get better after they are on your payroll. If their very best is 'on the border,' you would be best served to continue looking for the right people to fill your positions.

"Take it from me, a voice of experience. Never lower your standards just to fill a position! You'll pay for it later."

He paused and glanced at his watch, somewhat surprised.

"It seems like we just got started, but I see our time is

up for today. So tell me, what are you going to do differently during this coming week?"

"Well, first I'm going to slow down the hiring process and do it right," I promised. "My goal is to hire tough and make it an honor for someone to be on our team. I'm going to prepare every question and the ideal answer so that I know specifically what I'm looking for in each candidate and evaluate him or her as objectively as possible.

"Next, I'm going to involve Lynn and one of my superstars in the process, and I'm going to follow the Three Rules of Three so that I have enough information to make the best decision and hire tough.

"I know this is the most important decision I'll make for my team," I said, "and I'm going to do my very best to make a great decision."

"You're a good student, Jeff," Tony said, "and I can feel your enthusiasm about your opportunity to bring some new people to your team. Just remember, hire tough!"

"See you next week!"

Hire Tough

The most important asset in my organization is having the right people on my team.

What I see in an interview is the very best behavior of the person . . . it will not get any better.

It's important to follow the Three Rules of Three: three candidates, three times, three people evaluate.

I should never lower my standards just to fill a position! I will pay for it later.

The Seventh Monday

Exits and Entrances

By this time, I so looked forward to my Monday Morning meetings with Tony that I was getting up much earlier . . . and feeling much better about so many aspects of what had once been disaster areas in my life, both at work and at home.

I pulled into Tony's driveway well before our meeting time, but when I rang the bell, Tony was as charming as always. "Good morning, Jeff. How are things going?" he said, after opening the door. "Make any progress filling your open positions?"

"I think I made some major progress, Tony," I said when Tony came into the library with our mugs of coffee. "Lynn and I interviewed all twenty candidates for the three open positions. It was pretty taxing, but Lynn provided me with a good process to follow and we have narrowed the twenty down to nine possible candidates. The final round of interviews is scheduled for Wednesday, Thursday, and Friday of this week. By our next meeting, I will have offered the jobs to the three best candidates.

"And I'll tell you—after our conversation last week, I'm taking the hiring process much more seriously," I confessed.

"Great." Tony chimed in. "Taking shortcuts in the hiring process often causes you to pay dearly in the long run."

Then he stopped and took a long look at me. "You know, you seem to be a little on edge this morning. Everything going okay at home?"

I blanched. "I didn't know I was so easy to read. Everything is fine at home, though. Thanks for asking. There are, however, some major changes going on at work. I wasn't going to bring this up because I didn't want to interrupt where we are going, but since you asked, we are about to go through some major organizational changes, and, quite frankly, I am apprehensive about any changes right now.

"I finally have my team focused on the main things, and I am afraid the changes will disrupt all the good stuff we have been doing. Here's how it looks from where I sit. When things settle down a little, someone always seems to think that it is time for another organizational change. I don't know all the changes that will be taking place, but I do know that Karen has a new senior vice president, and so I'm sure there will be changes all the way down the ranks.

"Tony, I know you've been through your share of organizational changes, so maybe we could spend some time talking about how to deal with these changes."

"That is right up my alley, Jeff. Organizational change is where I spend most of my time consulting, and it's an area I really enjoy. I've been through start-ups, upsizing, downsizing, reorganizing, and everything in between. The two major issues in organizations, regardless of size or industry, are how to deal with change and how to handle the communication issues that accompany change. We've talked a lot about communications, so maybe this is the right time for us to talk about change.

"But before I share some of my experiences, let me ask you a couple of questions. First, how do you feel about change, and why are you so stressed out over these changes?"

"Generally, I don't like change," I admitted. "Who does? I prefer to make minor adjustments to things that are going well as opposed to making change for the sake of change. I'm probably stressed out because I'm headed into an unknown area. I am not sure what is going to happen, who I am going to be working for, and where the focus will be for my team."

"The stress you're describing is perfectly normal and natural," Tony assured, "and while I don't have the answers for all of your unknowns, I do know the success of any change depends, in large measure, on your attitude about that change.

"One way to look at this change is that you are exiting a comfortable place and entering an area that could be the launching pad for you and your organization," Tony continued, taking care to reassure me every step of the way.

"You see, every time we go through an exit, whether it

is job related or personal, we are making an entrance into a new opportunity. The only way for you to enter into the next level of your career is to exit the current level. That's what organizational change does—it exits the status quo and enters into a new beginning.

"Henry Ford once said, 'One of the great discoveries a man makes, one of his great surprises, is to find he can do what he was afraid he couldn't do.' He was talking about exiting the comfortable and entering the uncomfortable—just about where you are right now."

I could tell Tony was definitely in his element as he continued. "It takes a lot of courage to lead a group of people through change. The dictionary says courage is 'the attitude of facing and dealing with anything recognized as dangerous, difficult, or painful instead of withdrawing from it.' Sounds a whole lot like leading people through change, doesn't it?" "That is amazing." I responded. "I had never connected change and courage, but that is exactly what I see right now—danger, difficulty, and pain—with the changes we may be making."

"Good work! I'm glad you see the connection between change and courage." Tony replied. "You cannot make changes without the courage to exit the familiar. I think it is also important to understand the relationship between courage and fear. For some, courage means not feeling fear at all. Mark Twain defined courage as 'resistance to fear, mastery of fear—not absence of fear.' We walk forward along a path, fear is there, too. We keep walking.

"Now, Jeff. What would you say is the opposite of courage?"

"I think 'cowardice,' or maybe 'fear.' "

"Sure, both of those answers could apply, but I think the most appropriate answer is conformity. Courage is having the guts and the heart to do things differently for the sake of progress. Improvement doesn't happen by taking the path of least resistance or conforming to the way things have always been done.

"It takes leadership and courage to lead people through change and maintain focus, even when you have doubts about your own ability.

"Have you ever heard the phrase 'The only constant is change.'

"I heard it a long time ago . . . and many times since, come to think about it," I replied.

"When do you think that phrase first appeared? Was it last year, two years ago, thirty years ago?"

"Well, I am not sure when, but it has been around for a while. I would say somebody like Benjamin Franklin probably came up with it."

"Actually, Heracleitus was the first person credited with saying, 'The only constant is change'—in 500 B.C. He probably didn't make it up. He probably got it off the side of a cave wall somewhere—in 500 B.C!

"Do you suppose he was envisioning the warp-speed changes in business we face today?" Tony asked rhetorically. "Probably not! Nevertheless, leading people through change almost two thousand years ago undoubtedly came with its own unique set of challenges and difficulties.

"We—all people—inherently resist change in varying degrees . . . and, clearly, the message of that historical figure is: Exit the ways of the past and enter the path toward improvement for the future.

"Can we improve without changing something? Does improvement come from just wanting improvement? Obviously not," Tony pointed out. "Change is as natural as breathing, yet many seem to prefer to take their last breath rather than embrace change that leads to improvement.

"Change involves exiting your comfort zone and trying something different—entering an opportunity to improve. Without change, we can all get stuck in a rut of doing the same things the same way. So why should we be surprised when we achieve the same result? That rut can eventually become a grave. Why? Because the only difference between a rut and a grave is the depth of the hole."

Tony stopped, sipped his coffee, and immediately headed for the kitchen for a warm-up. "I've really been on a roll," he apologized as he set down the two now-steaming mugs. Once settled in his chair, he was ready with his next question.

"Did you read the book *Who Moved My Cheese?*"

"Yes, I read it a few years ago," I replied, "and remember thinking while reading it that I was a little resistant to change."

"That was a good little book. I enjoyed it, too, but long before that book was written, I heard about a university experiment involving a mouse that correlated with human reaction to change.

"Follow me on this: Four tubes were laid, side by side, on the floor—only inches apart. A cube of cheese was placed in the second tube. A mouse was then released, and it immediately went to the first tube. Finding the tube empty, the mouse proceeded to the second tube. There he discovered and ate the cheese, which met his basic need for survival. The mouse then returned to his point of release.

"The next day the mouse followed the same routine by going to the empty first tube, eating cheese from the second tube, and returning to his point of release. He repeated the same routine for several days.

"Finally, realizing that he was wasting time by going to the first tube, the mouse began going directly to the second tube. Each time, he ate the cheese, met his need for survival, and went back. This routine also continued for several days.

"The scientists conducting the experiment then made one minor change and moved the cheese to the third tube. The mouse went directly to the second tube where his needs had always been met and there was no cheese. What do you think was the mouse's response?"

"He probably either went back to the first tube or back to where he started. That would be my guess anyway," I responded.

"Good try, but guess again," Tony insisted.

"Did he go to the third tube searching for the cheese?" I was guessing, but that was the only other alternative I could think of.

"That would have been a good choice, but that isn't what he chose to do. Instead, he stayed in the second tube, where his need for survival had always been met, and waited for the cheese to come back to him.

"If allowed, the mouse would have starved in that second

tube, waiting for the cheese instead of reacting to the change. Doesn't this sound like the human reaction to change? 'Let's wait,' they say. 'We have always done it this way, and it has always worked in the past!'

"Two things can be learned from this story:

"First, if the situation changes—even if your needs have always been met and you are comfortable with the old way—react to the change. All through your life you have seen things change and improve. We exited the time of VHS videotapes and entered the time of DVDs. We exited the period of manual typewriters and entered the computer era. We exited CDs and entered into iPod. We have exited wires and entered wireless."

"All of those were good changes," I agreed. "They did lead to improvement, but I think changes in technology are easier to adjust to than changes involving people."

"Change is not unique to technology. Look around. Look at the workplace . . . or your family and friends. For me, traditions are important, especially our family traditions. But as my family has grown up and my children have married, we have had to make adjustments to our traditions. And it looks like I'll be making more adjustments when this new grandbaby arrives. I can't worry about the changes, but I do have to adapt to them.

"If you are waiting for things to be like they used to be, you could wind up starving like the mouse, or you may be just plain miserable. When situations change, don't sit and wait—always be courageous enough to look for your cheese," Tony directed.

"It's a good lesson," I said, "one worth remembering."

"The second lesson to be learned from the mouse is that while your needs are being met, keep looking for ways to improve," Tony went on. "A whole block of cheese could have been in the fourth tube, yet the mouse would not have known because he was content having his basic needs met. The bottom line is, When things are going well, keep looking for more cheese.

"There's one absolute: Change is not going away. In fact, there will probably be more changes in the next ten years than there have been in the last fifty years. So be prepared. Your reaction to change and your leadership through change will have a major impact on your success and the success of your team."

Now it was my turn to respond. "I hear what you're saying, and I don't disagree in theory. But change is hard on everyone. The exit door is tough to get through sometimes, even though what we are entering may eventually make us better. I guess my question is, Why is change so difficult for people to embrace? Why can't we just accept that change will happen and that it may be the entrance into something great?"

"Good questions," Tony said. "The answer is the same for both: It is natural human tendency to resist change. Even the smallest of changes—like sitting at a different spot at the dinner table, or taking a different seat in church or synagogue—is resisted.

"Most people enjoy stability and comfort. Change typically represents the opposite—discomfort and instability—

and, believe it or not, very few people enjoy traveling into those regions. Just ask anyone trying to lose weight or to give up smoking.

"Regardless of how anyone feels about it," Tony continued, "change is necessary for improvement. Someone once said: 'Insanity is doing the same thing the same way you have always done it and expecting different results.' Believe it! We have all experienced this kind of insanity at one time or another.

Tony looked through a stack of papers on the table next to him. "Oh, here it is—here's what I was looking for.

"In my own experience, I've found that people resist change for five primary reasons," Tony said, handing me the piece of paper with the following:

"First, the change is out of their control—it represents the unknown. They did not create or ask for the change. Any time you feel you are not in control, you become stressed and you begin to resist. That is a natural response, and the faster you can change the unknown into the known, the better.

"Second, people do not understand why they are changing. Without understanding why a change is being made, emotions tied to the old way of doing things are difficult to loosen. People have to understand why change is necessary before they are willing to let go of the past. Even if they do not agree, they will accept change more rapidly if they know why the change is occurring.

"Third, they succeeded the old way. In every organization, there is always a group of people who have excelled under the old conditions. Therefore, they don't feel the need to change—even though it may eventually make them more efficient . . . and make their work easier. So you can wind up with a group of strong resisters and a group of lukewarm (at best) supporters—both of whom you must lead and influence. Not an easy job. Talk with these folks. Acknowledge their past successes. Let them know how important they are to you and the team. Tell them you need their help . . . you need them to assume leadership roles in making the change happen.

"Fourth, they feel they are incapable of change. Changes in technology create fear for two reasons—one, because people are not confident they can learn the new technology and, two, because they are threatened by the change. Your role is to create confidence in your people and their ability to adjust to the change.

"Fifth, people think the price they have to pay outweighs the reward. Be aware. They may think the change is not worth the discomfort. Then, if they do not understand the result or like what they see, they will do anything to make the change fail.

"As a manager, you can help determine your team's enthusiasm for the change by focusing on the entrance of potential while you are working through the exit of the past."

"That's a tall order," I responded.

"Indeed." Tony smiled. "Did you ever walk into a movie, only to see the last ten minutes of the show as the hero and heroine head into the sunset and their life of happiness? All you saw was the outcome. Now, if you were to watch the same movie from the very beginning, your perception is completely different because you know what happens in the end. Your stress level is down, you can relax, and you can enjoy the trials they experience along the way, knowing that, in the end, there will be a storybook ending.

"As you lead your people through whatever changes are in the works, keep focused on the result. Talk about the rewards and see change as a leadership challenge. You may be entering the greatest time of your career."

I nodded my understanding.

"Well, Jeff. We are about out of time, but tell me, what are you going to do differently?"

"First, thanks for helping me look at change a little differently," I began. "I now see the connection between change, courage, and improvement, and I'll try to convey that to my team. From experience, I know leading people through change can be stressful, but now I have to focus on the end result and prepare to enter a new era if that is what is going to happen.

"I may meet resistance at every point in the process, but as the leader, my job is to stay at least one step ahead of the resisters . . . and, as Heracleitus said, Change is here to stay, so I need to embrace it because when I stop changing, I stop improving."

Tony looked pleased. "Exactly—and good luck this week. I am looking forward to next Monday and hearing what has happened."

Exits and Entrances

The success of change is largely determined by my attitude about change.

Change allows us to exit the comfortable and enter the improved.

People will resist change. I have to understand that and help them move positively through the change.

Do Less or Work Faster

Tony was anxiously awaiting my arrival on the eighth Monday. "Jeff, I couldn't wait to see you. Last week you were so stressed over the organizational changes. I was hoping you survived," he said as he poured coffee. "How did it go?"

"Well, believe it or not, there have not been any changes other than Karen's boss. It seems as though the new senior vice president is going to take his time evaluating the situation before he makes any major moves. I must say, I'm relieved, but when the changes eventually happen, I will be better prepared to exit the old and enter the new."

Tony was quick to jump in the conversation, "I think your senior vice president sounds very wise. I have seen too many executives go down in flames by making changes without understanding the situation and without having developed trust among the troops. So that is a good thing. Your exit and entrances will come later . . . and how is everything else?"

"Everything is going pretty smoothly, but this hiring process has been so time-consuming, I've barely had time to get anything else done . . . and that's another issue I wanted your insights on—how do I get everything done?

"Even though I think I've made a lot of progress during our sessions, it seems my time continues to be consumed by things outside my control. It's frustrating because I want to spend more time with my team . . . and my family," I explained.

"Jeff, you're sounding a lot like you did in our first meeting: 'Woe is me . . . I have no control over my time.' Well, it's possible you may be blaming your personal time-management problem on things outside your control. Let me ask you this: Who can spend your time but you?"

"Aren't you being a little harsh?" I countered defensively. "I simply said I seem to be consumed by things I feel I don't have much control over, and so I'm not able to do the important things I need—and want—to do."

"Sorry if I came across harshly," Tony apologized. "I'm trying to make a point. Your time is your responsibility. No one else can accept that responsibility for you. If you aren't able to do the important things, then you're the only one who can make adjustments to solve that problem. Your team is depending on you to be there for them, and that includes solving your personal time-management problems.

"First off, you need to assume control of the situation. One of the major sources of stress, anxiety, and unhappiness comes from feeling like your life is out of control. You need to figure out how to take control of your time so that you can take control of your life.

"Of course, there are some things we can't change about the way we spend our time," Tony admitted. "We have to wait in lines, at red lights, for elevators; there's not much we can do about those things. However, there is a lot we can do about situations at work.

"Jeff, I've studied time management for years—in fact, it's one of my favorite pastimes—and I've discovered that there are no magic bullets when it comes to time management." He continued, "I've never found anyone who had two or three hours a day they could save by doing one thing better. But I have seen many people find an hour or two a day they could use better by doing a few things differently.

Tony had my undivided attention because my time-management skills—or lack of them—had been a challenge since my college days.

"If you want to make better use of your time, you need to be looking for the small increments of time . . . a minute here, five minutes there, etc. Add them all up, and you'll create more time to use for other activities.

"I have also found the job seldom overworks the person," Tony said, "but people often overwork themselves by making bad time-management decisions. Bottom line, most people can't solve their time problem by working harder. Doing the wrong thing more or harder doesn't help. What we need to do is to find ways to shorten tasks, eliminate steps, combine some tasks, and work easier while getting other tasks done.

"One thing you have to remember is that no one can save time . . . we all have the same amount, and we can't carry any time over to the next day. Keeping these limitations in mind, we have to make better decisions on how we spend our time.

"I know of only two ways to spend time better. You can do less, or you can do everything faster. Those are our *only* choices. Of course, there are some things we could eliminate and just say no to. But for today's session, let's say the only option we have is to work faster. So how can you work faster? That's the question we need to address."

I scribbled down the question and awaited the answers.

"What are the time robbers you have to battle every day?" Tony asked.

Without having the real facts of the situation, I had to give Tony my best guess. "I think the major time robber for me is interruptions. It seems as though I am continually interrupted by people needing information that only I can provide. Also, the mounds of paperwork I have, and, of course, all the meetings I have to attend take a lot of time."

"So what percent of your time is wasted due to the interruptions, paperwork, and meetings?" Tony wanted to know.

"I'm not sure. I just know it's a lot. Sometimes it seems like those three things take up much of my day," I answered as honestly as I could.

"Your situation is similar to how other busy people feel," my mentored assured. "You go home at the end of the day, exhausted after working hard, and you are not sure where the time went.

"So the first thing you need to figure out is where your time is currently being spent: Get the facts. If you want to make improvements and become a better time manager, you've got to know where to start and what to improve. To find those answers, I suggest you track your time for two weeks so you can make some educated decisions about what to improve.

"You will find time is taken by the things we do and how we do things. Follow me on this," Tony prompted. "We spend our time doing the main things or doing the wrong things . . . and we spend our time doing things right or doing things wrong.

"For example, here's a chart, showing the four choices of how we can spend our time in a meeting:

How We Do the Things We Do

The Things We Do	Main Things Right	Main Things Wrong
	EXAMPLE: Run a productive and necessary meeting.	EXAMPLE: Waste two hours during an important meeting.
	Wrong Things Right	Wrong Things Wrong
	EXAMPLE: Facilitate a great meeting that was not necessary.	EXAMPLE: Waste everyone's time at an unnecessary meeting.

"Everything we do can be categorized into one of those four choices. If you keep track for two weeks, you'll know what you can do to make some better decisions," Tony pointed out, "and since you've already identified the main things in your department, I want you to classify your activities—are you doing those main things and how well are you doing them?

"Most executives have three areas—the same areas you identified—where they can make changes that will lead to major time improvements: prioritizing/organizing, interruptions, and meetings.

"While preparing for a speech a couple of weeks ago, I created a list of the best tips I've found about managing my time in each of those areas. Grab your pen and get ready to write. I am going to give you the best time-management tips I know. Pay attention, and you can change your life."

I was ready with my pencil and notepad.

"Let's talk about prioritizing and organizing first.

"Have you ever heard of the Pareto principle?" Tony asked.

"Yes, I know about the Pareto principle. When I was in sales, I was told that 20 percent of our customers would provide 80 percent of our results. My manager said that was the Pareto principle, or the 80/20 rule. I'm not sure why it was called the Pareto principle," I said, feeling pretty good that I finally knew the answer to one of Tony's questions.

"Your sales manager was right. But, the Pareto principle is broader than just sales. An Italian economist in the 1800s named Vilfredo Pareto discovered the principle when he observed that 20 percent of the people in Italy controlled 80 percent of the wealth. Then he began looking around and discovered that the 80/20 rule applied to many things. Today it is widely accepted that the Pareto principle applies in many areas of business, like 80 percent of your

results will come from 20 percent of your activities, 80 percent of your complaints will come from 20 percent of your
customers, and so on. It definitely applies to time management, as well.

"There are a few things that you can do that will yield
better results than your doing a whole lot of other things,"
Tony explained, "and it's your duty to yourself and your
team to know where your highest payoff activities are and
eliminate the activities that yield the fewest results. If you
can concentrate your time and energy on your most important task, do it well, and complete the task, then you will be
successful. If you spend your time on things that are not important, do a halfway job, or never complete tasks, you will
not be successful.

"Jeff, here is an interesting quiz," Tony said, changing
his tone. "Let's suppose you have five tasks that need to be
accomplished today. Using the Pareto principle, one of
those tasks will generate 80 percent of your results. Which
one of the tasks do you think the average person would do
first?"

"Obviously the one that gets the most results would be
the task I would do first," I replied. "Why not?"

"That's a great answer, Jeff, but the task most people
are likely to procrastinate on is the most important task—
probably because it's often the toughest task to complete.
They stay busy with all the other tasks, save the most important, then wind up accomplishing very little. Now, if
you were really doing what you said—completing first the
task that generates 80 percent of your results—I doubt that

we would be having this conversation on time management."

"You've got me there." I confessed.

Tony continued, "Prioritizing is where time management begins. Select your most important task for that particular moment and get it done quickly and well. Many people become stressed over what they have to do instead of getting things done. Always ask yourself, What is the most important use of my time right now?, and get started. Starting and completing important tasks first will eliminate stress and help you to feel good about yourself and the rest of the day.

"One of the most important activities for me is to set aside some uninterrupted planning time every day," Tony said. "It was difficult for me to discipline myself to do this, but I found that in twenty *uninterrupted* minutes, I could get the same amount accomplished that would have taken sixty minutes of *interrupted* time. If you can't set aside twenty minutes, maybe you can set aside ten. That's still a great return on your time investment.

"Just close your door and think about what needs to be done and in what order. It will make a huge difference in defining your focus for the day," he suggested.

"That sounds reasonable, but how can I set aside uninterrupted time when I can't get everything I need done now?" I said.

"I guess that's a good question, Jeff, but it doesn't make sense to me. If you plan for ten minutes, you can accomplish thirty minutes of productivity. Wouldn't that be worth it? In reality, you will never have enough time to do everything you need to do, so what you need is a crystal-clear understanding of the important things you have to do.

"You can know that only when you have some uninterrupted time to think about what needs to be accomplished and then begin doing it. Try it. You will discover that the payoff is immediate," Tony promised.

"Now let's get to the paperwork issue. Like many, you probably think you are the only person feeling bogged down by paperwork. Here's my solution: Some paperwork is important and would be considered a main thing. But other paperwork could be eliminated, and no one would know the difference. Executives have to figure out ways to get the important paperwork done faster and quickly maneuver through the paperwork hindering us from getting important things done.

"Every time-management guru I know will tell you to touch paper only once. Actually, I think the key to taking control of your paperwork is to keep the paper moving. Throw it away, act on it, or put it into your reading pile. Do something with the paper instead of shuffling it. It may not be reasonable to touch paper only once in every situation, but remember—shuffling and reshuffling paper from pile to pile with no evaluation or action is a waste of time.

"Would it surprise you that a lot of the paperwork you have to deal with is not needed?" Tony asked.

I nodded in the affirmative.

"Well, I suggest you conduct an audit on every report that hits your in-box. Is the report really necessary? If not, eliminate it. If you need only one line item off a report, ask the originator of the report to send you just that line item.

"One more thing, Jeff. If I were to walk into your office right now, what would I see on the top of your desk?" Tony asked.

"Let's see. I have not been there since Saturday morning, but I think I have several piles of paper on my desk. You would probably describe my desk right now as cluttered."

"When you get back to your office today, first thing, clear off the top of your desk. I think you should always be able to see the majority of your desk's surface. Don't fool yourself into thinking that a cluttered desk makes you look important. Quite the contrary. A cluttered desk makes you look disorganized and contributes to the shuffling and reshuffling game. It also adds stress. At a minimum, your desk should be completely clean at the end of every day."

I nodded, somewhat embarrassed about what I would be walking into when I returned to my office.

"Another organizational tip is to batch activities—do like activities together—so that you're not starting and stopping all the time. Do all your voice mails at once. Return all phone calls at one time. Write memos or letters at one sitting," said Tony.

"One batching opportunity for almost everyone is e-mail. You can control your e-mail deliveries and responses by doing them a few times a day, as opposed to all through the day. I hope you're not one of those people who check their e-mail every ten minutes. I receive a lot of e-mail every day. In fact, I could be at my computer all day, just responding to e-mail. Don't get me wrong. I've embraced this technology as one of the best tools we could have, but I work my e-mail deliveries into my personal schedule so that they don't control my day. After all, you don't go to the post office every ten minutes, do you?

"Here are a couple of other tips for e-mail management. First, save all of your e-mail except spam and other things that are not important to your business. File them on an external disk, just in case you ever need to retrieve something. Second, keep your in-box empty. Do something—file, delete, or act upon—every e-mail you receive. Don't just let them pile up in your in-box. It adds stress and unnecessary frustration when you open up your e-mail and find tons of messages sitting there.

Tony continued. "Let me ask you another question. How often do you call Karen or the people on your team?"

"In most cases, when something comes up, I call them immediately and take care of it right then. That sounds like something you would be pleased with, eh?" I responded, thinking I was finally doing something in a productive mode.

"Well, the immediate call is good on critical items, and maybe all of your responses are critical. But maybe you can eliminate interrupting them if you create a 'talk to' file for Karen and every person on your team. Unless it is a real emergency, wait until you have at least two items in the file before calling that person and ask both questions at the same time. That could save you and the person you are calling half the time.

"The key to batching is to eliminate as many transitions from one activity to another as possible. I assure you, if you batch activities together, you can save ten to twenty minutes a day.

"Okay, let's go to another area. When do you normally take off for lunch?" Tony asked.

"I try to go around noon. That way, I get to see most of the people on my team and eat with some of them."

"That's great that you get to eat with folks on your team. But here's a simple tip that can give you ten, maybe fifteen minutes every day. Go to lunch at eleven or one. Why everyone decides to go to lunch at noon is a mystery to me," Tony said, scratching his head. "They wait on the elevator, wait in line at the deli, wait in line to get back on the elevator, and then complain about not having enough time for lunch. Make the same suggestion to your team, and you can still have time for them; and every one of you will save ten or fifteen minutes."

I made a note. That was an excellent suggestion.

"Now, let's talk about another key area of time management—interruptions. Where do most of your interruptions come from?"

"I would say the majority come from customers, followed by phone calls, my team, and Karen," I said, although I did not have any facts to back up my assumption and hoped Tony would not ask for more detail.

"Great," he responded, much to my relief. "Most people don't know who is interrupting them or why they're being interrupted. You seem to have a good feel for it, but just for a week or so, keep track of who is interrupting you and why they're interrupting. Then you can make some informed decisions about how you're going to address the problem. Of course, the customer interruptions are a necessary part of the job, but you may discover that you have other consistent interrupters you can address.

"In my own experience, I've found that even if you can't eliminate the interruption," Tony said, "you can keep it short. Try to make all of your phone calls shorter and straight to the point.

"If someone comes into your office and interrupts what you are doing, I have discovered that, as a general rule, the length of the interruption is in direct proportion to the comfort level of the interrupter. The secret is not allowing the interrupter to sit down and get comfortable in your office. When someone comes into your office, stand up. You can take care of business standing up more quickly than—and just as well as—sitting down."

That point hit home to me. "That's pretty interesting. I know you are right because I do stand up occasionally when people pop in. My desk faces the door, and a lot of people walk right in, regardless of what I have going on."

"You may want to think about turning your desk to face away from the door," Tony suggested. "The way your furniture is arranged can invite interruptions and steal some time from you. I would arrange your office furniture so that your desk doesn't face the flow of traffic. If you're looking at every person who walks down the hall, and everyone thinks they would be rude by not saying hello to you, you could be wasting a lot of time without even knowing it.

"Another good management practice is to schedule

one-on-one sessions at least monthly with your staff and your boss. Gather everything you need to talk about and take care of it all at one sitting rather than interrupting one another the minute something comes up. It also forces you to communicate regularly, which would eliminate some of the issues you were facing with Karen.

"Finally, you may want to ask your team this: What do I do that wastes your time and hinders your performance? Some of their suggestions may surprise you and could save you and your team valuable time.

"Now, before we leave this discussion, let's talk about one of the biggest time wasters I know—meetings. On your team's survey, several of your team members mentioned that they thought your meetings were not extremely productive. If that is the case, you are not alone.

"Jeff, I've been to a gazillion meetings in my day and have found that—if everyone is prepared, on time, and focused—most meetings can be accomplished in half the time meetings are currently taking. Here's a scary statistic: The average person wastes about 250 hours per year in unproductive meetings. That's a lot of time and money being wasted!

"Here's another alarming fact. Meetings are expensive, probably the largest expense that does not have a line item on the income statement. Think about it. A one-hour meeting of a dozen executives could cost $5,000 or more. Make your meetings productive but short.

"Your team could give you some great suggestions on how they think your meetings could be improved, and I would listen to them. Allow them to take ownership of making your meetings better. But, since they are not here this morning, here are some suggestions to improve meeting productivity:

"First, don't fall into the 'perpetually scheduled meeting' syndrome where you're having meetings just because meetings are regularly scheduled. Make sure every meeting is absolutely necessary. Routine meetings are not a good investment unless they are helping you accomplish your objectives. Remember, keep the main things the main things.

"Always begin a meeting by covering the most important items. That way you ensure that you cover what you need to accomplish, and you're not rushing through the important items. Start with the most important and work your way toward the least important items on the agenda. If you're spending thousands of dollars on a meeting, it is probably not a good investment to solve a hundred-dollar problem. Focus on what is important and keep moving through your agenda."

Tony's points were ones I wanted to incorporate immediately. The comments from my team on the most recent survey still had a certain sting to them. I really wanted to improve.

Tony had another question. "Tell me what happens when someone comes in ten minutes late to one of your meetings? What if Kevin, one of your middle stars, is the one who shows up late? How do you handle it?"

"If Kevin was running late, which would be really unusual, I would probably wait on him for ten minutes before I started the meeting. If the meeting has already started, I would go over what we had already covered to get him up to speed as fast as I could," I answered.

Tony was quick to jump in. "That is what most people do, particularly with their superstars or middle stars. Be careful with that strategy because you are sending a message to the people who showed up on time that they are not as important as Kevin," he said.

"My suggestion is to start your meeting on time and avoid the temptation of recapping when someone shows up late. When you recap, you're rewarding the tardy person and punishing the people who were on time. There should be accountability with your meetings with a penalty for showing up late. Reward the people who made it on time with a well-planned, productive session.

"Probably the simplest tip that pays the biggest dividend in meeting management is to start and end your meetings on time. It's disrespectful and a bad investment to start a meeting later than scheduled. You waste thirty minutes of productivity by beginning a meeting with ten people three minutes late. Think about that. If your meeting is scheduled to end at three, once you hit one minute after, everyone begins looking at their watches, wondering how much longer the meeting will last. You can rest assured that your productivity has gone out the window when the scheduled meeting time has passed.

"Another meeting time waster is allowing people to continue to 'sell' their points after a decision has been made. Some folks like fighting losing battles. Don't fall for that. Set limits on the time allowed per item and move forward.

"What about lunch meetings?" Tony wanted to know.

"I rarely call lunch meetings with my team but I am asked to attend lunch meetings quite often," I allowed. "When I see an agenda, I always look to see who is scheduled over lunch. That tells me who is considered the least important presentation on the agenda."

"You're exactly right." Tony agreed. "The person presenting over lunch will not receive much attention. My general rule is, 'Never eat and meet.' You either eat *or* you meet, but you can't do both well. If the presentation is worth spending time on, people should be attending to *it*, not the salad or whatever they are eating. It would be better to have a thirty-minute lunch break for everyone to take a breather, anyway.

"As a sidebar on food, if your meeting continues after lunch, do not cater turkey for lunch. Turkey contains chemicals that are natural sedatives, which is not what you need when everyone needs to be focused and at their best.

"The last area I want to talk about is your personal time. I have seen many executives burn out because they try to accomplish an impossible task—getting everything done.

"Without question, you need to take time for yourself and your family. Get to bed early, work hard, but take at least one complete day off work every week . . . and commit to taking that vacation you've been putting off. Everyone needs rebooting once in a while.

"The paradox of time management," Tony said, "is that the more time you take off, the more refreshed you will be to get the important things accomplished. Your energy level will be greater, your attitude will be better, and the people around you will be more productive.

"You have the power to choose how you want to live every day," Tony continued. "You have the time and resources to accomplish what you want to accomplish. No one else can create time for you to get the important things done. You have to make the decision to do it yourself.

"These are just a few ideas to help you make better use of your time. There are many more," Tony said, "and I suggest you invest some time in reading a book on time management and look for several other areas where you can gain a few extra minutes every day.

"Speaking of time, our time is about up for this week," said Tony, following his own counsel. "So what are you going to do differently next week?"

"Well, I'm going to finish the hiring process," I replied. "That's the main thing of all main things this week. While you were talking, I was doing a mental self-check on the meetings I facilitate, and I know I can do a better job, creating some additional time for my team and myself. I'm also going to track who interrupts me and the number of times I interrupt others. I may be guilty of being the number-one interrupter of my team members. And I'm going to buy a book on time management, seeking other ideas to help me gain control of my time and my life."

"Great, Jeff!" Tony's enthusiastic response energized my own resolve. "Try out some of those ideas. I know you'll find some more time for yourself and your family."

"See you next week!"

Do Less or Work Faster

My time is my responsibility. I need to take control of my time so I can take control of my life.

I need to shorten my meetings by half.

I will keep track of how I spend my time for two weeks so I can make better decisions on what to eliminate or do faster.

I will look for small increments of time by prioritizing, limiting interruptions, and effectively managing meetings.

Buckets and Dippers

I arrived at Tony's promptly at eight-thirty A.M. He greeted me at the door.

"Jeff, how are you today and how was your week?" he wanted to know as he guided me into the library. "Did you make any progress filling your open positions? And how about your time management? Did you find any places where you could spend your time better . . . and, of course, I want to hear how the team is doing?"

I had spent the weekend looking forward to our Monday morning conversation. "Last week was a much better week. Lynn and I completed the interviewing and made job offers to the best three candidates," I said.

"Two of them accepted and will report to work in a couple of weeks. One person turned us down and decided to stay at his current company. I was going to offer the job to our next best candidate, but Mark (one of my superstars who helped interview) said the next best candidate didn't fit well with our team, so he suggested we keep looking for a more qualified candidate.

"Since you said to hire tough and never lower my standards, I asked Lynn to begin the process of finding the right person for our last open position . . . and yes, I'm really excited about the two new team members.

"I also tried several of your time-management tips. I kept a log of where I was spending my time and discovered I was spending a lot of time on things that weren't important. I also found one particular person in our office interrupted me at least six times a day. I showed her my log of how many times we were talking to each other in a day, and she couldn't believe she called me that often.

"After our mutual discovery, we made a deal to talk at ten A.M. and three P.M. only. I guess you would call that 'batching.'

"I also cut our weekly team meeting time in half. We normally allow an hour for our meeting, and we always seem to go the full hour, whether we need to or not. This week, I said we needed to cover everything faster so we could be finished in thirty minutes. Well, you know what? We did it. We started with our most important items and finished them all.

"That gave everyone on the team an extra thirty minutes that day, which we used for uninterrupted planning.

"We wanted to test your theory of accomplishing what would normally take us ninety minutes to do in thirty minutes of uninterrupted time. I guess I shouldn't have been surprised, but the theory worked! Some of my cynical troops weren't sure we accomplished in thirty minutes what normally took us ninety, but everybody agreed we at least doubled our productivity in those thirty minutes. What a bonus—for everyone!

"See, Tony. I really was listening last week, and those were some great ideas. I do feel like I'm more in control of my time now, but I still have a way to go. I also bought a book on time management to read . . . when I find the time."

"So now you're a comedian?" Tony chuckled. "But seriously. You made some great choices last week, and it sounds as though the new people have the talent as well as the desire to be on your team. Plus, you made some better choices in how you spent your time. Good job!

"If I were you, I would approach Chad and Jeni about your last, remaining open position," he continued. "You already know they're superstars and will fit in with your team. Undoubtedly, you may have to swallow your pride when you ask them to come back, but I think it's a good idea. You may find that one of them would be happy to come back to your organization.

"Now, I want you to look in your spiral notebook at the notes you made when you talked to Chad and Jeni. They mentioned three things they expected from you. What were they?"

"Well, let's see," I said, leafing back to the front of the book. "They said they wanted me to hire good people, coach every member of the team to become better, and dehire the people who aren't carrying their share of the load. Is that what you were asking?"

"Yes," said Tony, and how have 'we' done in those three areas?"

"I think I've made great progress in hiring other good people to be on the team," I answered. "Tony, you've taught me well, and I'm now hiring tough. Lynn from HR also was a great support throughout the process, and I really feel good about the two new people who are coming on board.

"As far as coaching every team member to become better, I think I've made a little headway. I'm paying more attention to the superstars and middle stars, but I'll have to admit, I really haven't focused very much on coaching my good performers.

"Of course, I had to dehire Todd. Amazingly, I thought he was a superstar until I found out others on the team were covering for him. I guess that just proves I was spending too much time in management land.

"Before I begin more dehiring, though, I need to better define my expectations and ensure that the proper training and tools are in place. Through this entire process, I discovered the performance reviews I've been giving don't accurately reflect performance, so I may have a lot more work to do in the dehiring area."

"Well, Jeff, it sounds as though you're at least making progress in addressing the three things Chad and Jeni suggested. Great job," my mentor said encouragingly.

"For the remainder of our time today, I would like to focus on how you can coach every member of the team to become better. Now, I'm not talking about performance improvement sessions. I'm talking about recognition of, and communication with, everyone on the team.

"A few weeks ago we talked about a place called management land and how sometimes we get caught up in the things happening in management land while we overlook important things on the team, remember?

"Well, here are two facts you should never forget, regardless of your title or position:

"First, your leadership success is the cumulative results of your team. You cannot be successful without your team being successful. You are needed and you are important, but you get paid for what your team does more than what you do.

"Second, you need your team more than your team needs you.

"Don't get me wrong, Jeff. You all need each other, but cumulatively, the seventeen people on your team accomplish much more than you do."

Tony had a way of cutting to the chase, sometimes more quickly than my ego could endure.

"To make my point, answer a couple of questions. First, what percentage of the work that needs to be done is getting done while you're here meeting with me this morning?"

As always, Tony's questions zinged to the bull's-eye of the issue. "Well, er, I think or I hope they're getting about 95 percent of the work accomplished, even while I'm not there," I stumbled.

"Okay, I would agree. Ninety-five percent is probably an accurate number. Some of your people may say 105 percent—because they think they get more done while you're away—which may nor may not be so, but let's go with your 95 percent.

"Now, let's suppose your seventeen people were here with me and you were the only one left at the office. What percentage of the work would be getting done then?" Tony asked.

"Not much! I would probably get about 10 percent of the work done," I responded as honestly as I could.

"So your team is accomplishing 95 percent, and you can only accomplish 10 percent? Then who needs who the most? Obviously you need one another, but never forget that your job is to help all your team members become better at the job they've chosen. They have entrusted a portion of their life to you, and it's your job to help them grow, personally and professionally. That means you need to do everything you can to help them become the very best!

"Follow me on this analogy: Every person has a bucket of motivation. That bucket can be filled to overflowing, or it can be empty and desperately in need of filling. Sometimes the buckets have leaks . . . and those buckets lose motivation as fast as you can try to motivate.

"Every person also has a dipper," Tony continued. "In fact, some people have these great big, long dippers they enjoy putting into other people's buckets. Those big, long dippers represent cynicism, negativism, confusion, stress, doubt, fear, anxiety, and any other thing that can drain someone's desire and motivation.

"As a leader, your job is to keep everyone's bucket filled. You are the chief bucket filler, and the best way to fill

buckets is with excellent communication and encouragement. In fact, there are four things you really have to do if
you're going to keep your team members' motivation buckets full:

"First, a full bucket requires knowing the main things
important to doing a good job. We talked about this before,
and you and your team have now identified the main things.
But if people don't know what the main thing is, their motivation bucket will leak like a water bucket full of shotgun
holes. A leader with focus and direction fills buckets. A leader
who creates confusion and inconsistency has a big, long dipper that drains people's buckets.

"Second, to keep buckets filled, you need to *provide the
bucket holders with feedback* on how they're doing. You may
think a performance appraisal will keep a bucket full, but it
won't. Performance appraisals may fill a bucket for a short
period of time, but the bucket will have leaks in it after a few
days. Don't get me wrong—performance reviews are important and necessary to document performance, but they don't
provide long-term motivation.

"People need to know how they're doing all the time,
not just at performance-review time. But here's a warning:
You can have great intentions to fill buckets and yet be draining those very buckets if you don't follow the rules of effective feedback . . . and they are the following:

"One: Be sincere. If you're not sincere about your
feedback, people will see through you like a crystal glass. In-
sincere feedback is a great big dipper into someone's bucket.
Giving positive feedback can backfire if it's perceived as not

being genuine. Most people are experts, or at least think they are, at reading the sincerity of their manager. Faking positive feedback is risky. Be sincere . . . or wait until you can be.

"Two: To fill buckets, your feedback has to be specific. If you're not specific with your praise, the bucket will not fill up. Why? Because the bucket holder will tip over the bucket while scratching his or her head, wondering what you're talking about." Tony laughed at his own humor then reinforced his point. "If you just tell someone 'good job on your project report' that is okay, but what behavior would you want them to repeat . . . specifically, what constituted a 'good job.' Instead, if you tell them, 'Thanks for your excellent detailed report on the project; I especially liked the way you outlined the action plan required for next week,' then you have filled his bucket and told her what is specifically important to you. The words 'I especially liked' are great words to begin your specific feedback.

"Three: Feedback must be timely. The quicker you give feedback after the behavior you're trying to reinforce, the better your results will be. The more time you wait to fill the bucket, other people's dippers will get into the bucket. Then you'll have to work twice as hard to fill it back up.

"And Four: Feedback must be aligned with the receiver's value system. Don't try to fill someone's bucket with something that's important to you but not to him.

"I learned this a few years ago when I 'rewarded' one of my top performers with my thirty-yardline tickets to a conference championship football game. Those tickets were important to me . . . really important . . . but the game was on the same day as Huntleigh and Kim's wedding. Obviously, I was not going to miss the wedding! Anyway, I gave my tickets away to Shawn Garner, one of my top employees.

"I didn't realize it at the time, but Shawn was not a football fan. As unbelievable as it was to me, he did not even know the game was scheduled. He went to the conference championship, but it did not mean much to him. Come to find out, he was a movie buff and he would have been happier if I had given him tickets to a movie premier. It would have cost me a lot less, and he would have had a lot more fun.

"The lesson? Bucket filling is in the eye of the bucket holder, not the bucket filler. Fill their buckets with things that are important to *them* . . . not you.

"Another point to remember in keeping your team members' buckets filled is to let them know you care about them and the job they do. One of the basic human needs is to be appreciated.

"I had a peer once tell me that most of the time what prevents people from accomplishing their goals is not the mountain ahead, but the small grain of sand in the shoe. Many times the grain of sand is the lack of attention from the person who is supposed to be leading them. Some people are so focused on the big things that they forget to take care of the basics, such as taking time to show their team they sincerely care about them. Showing you care does not require money or much time . . . it only requires your focus and attention.

"There are a gazillion ways to show you care and fill your team's buckets. Of course, the paycheck they get fills their buckets to some degree, but those buckets will dry up if you only bucket fill on days you hand them a paycheck. Find those bucket fillers that work best with your team, and then use them to fill their buckets often.

"Here are a few ways to show your team members you care about them—they seem to work well for other bucket fillers I know:

Involve people in major decisions.

Listen to them—they often have the best ideas anyway.

Memorize facts about the bucket holder and his or her family.

Most people enjoying sharing their family weekend experiences. Let them fill their own buckets while you listen.

Make coffee for your team. Making coffee is a pretty simple act that people appreciate—it's an easy bucket filler.

Send thank-you notes to team members at home. People normally get only bills and junk mail at home. A positive note of recognition goes a long way to filling a bucket.

Send bucket holders a Thanksgiving card. Your
success is dependent on them—who else at
work would you be more thankful for?

Ask your superstars—if they're interested—to
become mentors for middle stars or falling
stars. This is a win/win—everyone's bucket gets
filled.

Keep a camera at the office to record significant
bucket-filling events at company activities.

Plant a tree on company property in honor of
your team.

Create a library of books, tapes, and magazines,
and keep it current and well stocked so team
members can fill their own buckets.

Create a "wall of fame" with pictures of your
team members and their families.

Follow the platinum bucket-filling rule: Treat
people the way they wish to be treated.

Spend time with all your team members.
Sometimes simply being around and showing
that you care about them will automatically fill
their buckets.

**Finally, know how well the team is doing.
Everyone wants to be on a winning team. Make
sure team members consistently know whether
the team is winning or not.**

"If you will fulfill these bucket-filling requirements—
know the main things, give feedback on performance, provide recognition for doing a good job, and communicate
the team score—your team members will be asking you
what they can do to help fill your bucket. That's the way it
works. The more buckets you fill, the more your bucket is
filled.

"One of the greatest things you can do for yourself and
others is to encourage people by lifting them up and helping
them," Tony explained. "It is easy—and maybe natural—to
discourage others. The world is full of discouragers, so no
more discouragement is needed. Instead, make it your personal mission to encourage others. If you do, your bucket
will never go dry."

Tony glanced at his watch. "Well, once again, our time is
up," he said, always ending our meetings on time. "But, before
you go, tell me what you're going to do before next week?"

"Several things," I said as I flipped through my notes.
"First, I'm going to call Jeni and Chad to see if one of them
is interested in returning to the team. I'm going to share with
them the changes I'm making, and will continue to make, to
become a better leader.

"I really like your bucket-filling analogy. In fact,
I'm going to share it with my team. If we can keep our

dippers out of one another's buckets, I think we can all be more motivated, productive, and happy. I may even give them a bucket and dipper to drive home the analogy, just for fun," I said.

"Great plan, Jeff, and good luck with Jeni and Chad. I hope that works out well for you. Our nine sessions so far have been a great experience for me."

"For you?" I said with surprise. "These sessions have been incredible for *me*. You've helped turn my career around, and I can see good things happening because you've taken the time to listen, emphasize, and direct me to improve. I can't thank you enough."

Tony smiled. "Well, they have been rewarding for me as well. Now, we have only one session remaining. During that session, I want to spend our time talking about you and what you can do to accomplish your personal goals. Next week, we'll talk about overcoming adversity—we all have to deal with adversity somewhere along the way, and I want to share some of my experiences in that area—and then we will finish our session by talking about your legacy.

"In the meantime, have a good week. I'll look forward to seeing you next Monday."

Buckets and Dippers

Ways I need to fill buckets: Know the main things, give feedback, provide recognition, keep score.

The more buckets I fill, the more my bucket will be filled.

I need to pay attention to what is important to my team members and reward them appropriately.

The Gift of Your Legacy

Welcome, Jeff. It's your graduation day." Tony beamed as we shook hands and headed for his library.

"The last time I went to your graduation, I told you that the learning was just beginning. The same thing applies now, even after all the years of experience you have. If the truth were known, I've probably learned more in our sessions than you have. Thank you for allowing me to share these Monday mornings with you."

"Wait! Don't thank me," I protested. "You gave your time and knowledge to *me*!"

I could tell Tony was uneasy with my praise.

"Well, enough of the boola-boola," he said, as he motioned for me to follow him to the kitchen. "But before you tell me about what happened at work last week, I have a few things I'd like to say . . . which is nothing unusual," he chuckled.

"First, I want to commend you. It took courage for you to call me several weeks ago. You might not have called unless you were at a point where you had nothing to lose, but you still had the courage to call. I understand that feeling of being at the end of your rope.

"I've been there before and made a similar call, out of the blue, to an old friend. If you hadn't had the courage to make the call, most likely nothing would have changed except you'd probably be even more frustrated. Anyway, I'm glad you called.

"I feel like I have gotten to know you very well during the past ten weeks, but I don't feel like I know your family," he said as he poured our coffee and we headed to the library. "I would love to take your family to dinner in the near future, if you're interested."

"That would be terrific! Let's plan on making that happen before the end of the month," I suggested.

"That's a deal," he said, taking a seat in his comfortable library. "So tell me, how did things go this week?"

"The best news is that Jeni is coming back to the company," I began. "I explained the changes I was making in my leadership to her. Then, I think she called several of her friends on the team to see if I was really doing what I had outlined in our conversation—and to find out if it was making a difference. On Wednesday, I got a call from her saying she really wanted to come back to the team, so she starts in two weeks. That's a real positive in my book."

Tony nodded his agreement. "That is good news."

"The new hires are doing great," I continued. "They're energetic, enthusiastic, and it's rubbing off on the rest of the team . . . including me. It was worth the time and effort to hire tough and get the right people on board.

"Remember your analogy of the bucket and the dipper? I shared that with the team. Then we brainstormed some of our own rules for bucket filling and what to do when someone gets his dipper in your bucket. Not only was it a fun exercise, it definitely made a point. A couple of times last week I heard people say, 'Get your dipper out of my bucket!' when a negative or cynical comment was made.

"And . . . that's about it. Things are going pretty smoothly, now that we have focus."

"Those are giant steps, Jeff," Tony commended. "Remember I told you our last session would be all about you?" Tony's tone was back to its serious pitch. "We've spent nine sessions talking about your team, your leadership style, and how to get results from others. Now let's focus on what you can do to achieve the goals you have for yourself."

I was focused. I needed to hear what Tony was about to say.

"Do you remember how you felt when we first started meeting?" Tony began. "I could tell you were apprehensive and somewhat cynical about even being here, but you were desperate and failing, so you were willing to try almost anything."

"I did not mean to come across as cynical about our meetings," I apologized, "but you're right. I was desperate, but I was also very appreciative you would even take the time to meet with me. Now, I'll admit I wasn't sure how things would go and if any improvements could be made, but I've been extremely pleased with our meetings . . . no, I've been blown away with your mentoring. You are pretty tough, but I have learned a lot!"

"Jeff, when we first began our meetings, you were missing something," Tony continued. "What was absent in your personal and professional life was a small thing that makes a big difference in achieving success. Your missing ingredient didn't cost a penny, but you didn't have it."

I was puzzled. "I guess I don't know what you're referring to." I finally managed to say. "Since our meetings, you have provided me with numerous skills that I've been able to use. You have given me a logical track to follow to improve my management skills. Are some of those skills what I was missing?"

"All of those skills are important," Tony agreed, "but what you were missing overrides all the skills you could learn—and that missing element was enthusiasm. You were beaten down to the point that you were unable to be enthusiastic about anything . . . and it was obvious to me and to everyone else. You were allowing your past failures to consume your future.

"Enthusiasm is something you can't fake, and it has a tremendous effect on everyone around you," Tony explained. "Let me give you an example. Once there was a salesman who moved into a new town and met an old-timer as he was leaving the bank. 'I'm new to your town. What are the people like here?' the salesman asked.

"'What were the people like in the town you came from?' the old-timer wanted to know.

"'Well, they were glum and negative and always complaining, and their glasses were always half empty,' the salesman replied.

" 'Hmmm,' said the old-timer. 'Sounds about like the people who live here.'

"A few weeks later, another person moved to the same town and met the same old-timer as he was leaving the same bank. 'I'm new to your town. What are the people like here?' the newcomer asked.

" 'What were the people like in the town you came from?' the old-timer responded.

" 'Well, they were wonderful. They worked together in the neighborhood, helped one another, and were always there to support us during tough times. We're going to miss them,' the newcomer replied.

" 'Hmmm,' said the old-timer. 'I think you will like it here, too. That sounds about like the people who live here.'

"The old-timer's message? If you want to be around people who are positive and enthusiastic and eager to live life, your attitude has to be the same. If you think the people around you are glum and negative, you probably need to check your attitude—because it's probably glum and negative, too.

"If you want to be around happier people, choose to be happy yourself. It all starts with you." Tony explained. "As an old farmer used to tell his children, 'You can't change the fruit without changing the root.' Our root is our attitude, and our fruit is how others see us.

"The longer we live and the older we get, the more evidence we have that our attitude impacts every aspect of our lives. If you look closely, you'll find attitude becomes the linchpin for your opportunities, your circumstances, your successes, and your failures," he said, nodding his head knowingly.

"I understand all of that, and I'm not arguing with you," I countered. "I know my attitude is reflected all around me. I certainly do not make a conscious choice to be negative, but, when you think about it, probably anyone in my circumstance would have been negative, too."

"So, do you think that your attitude is basically on autopilot," Tony wondered aloud. "When good things happen, you have a good attitude. When bad things happen, you have a bad attitude. Is that the way it works?"

"Well, yes, to a certain degree." I responded. "Who wouldn't be happy if everything he touched turned to gold?"

"Jeff, many people subscribe to the theory that attitudes are simply automatic responses to circumstances, that your attitude is simply a reflection of external circumstances. The automatic response to something negative is negative . . . and the automatic response to something positive is positive. Whatever happens to us dictates the way we respond."

I thought for a minute, but Tony interrupted the silence.

"Personally, I don't buy into that theory," he said. "Your attitude is completely *internally* controlled . . . a personal response to conditions and circumstances . . . no one can externally control your own attitude.

"Of course, all things that happen to us are not all within our control," Tony admitted, "but we do control how we respond to those events. We choose how we react . . . no one can make that choice for us. When you were in your slump, you chose to react like you had already lost the battle.

"Jeff, unfortunately, we don't live in a Pollyanna world where only good things happen to good people. Far from it . . . everyone has things happen that are unexpected and unpleasant, and we have to deal with those events. No, let me put that another way. We have to have the courage to deal with those events.

"We may not want to admit this responsibility, but the facts are clear: We are in charge of our attitudes—and our happiness. The choices about the attitude we'll embrace are choices we make every day and a choice we make many times a day.

"Your attitude is powerful," he said, stopping for a sip of coffee.

"Doctors confirm that the difference between those who survive a serious illness and those who do not survive is often the attitude of the patient. In sports, coaches will tell you the attitude of the team is a major portion of the game plan. In school, teachers have found that positive kids produce positive results. In business, a Gallup poll revealed that 90 percent of people said they were more productive when they were around positive people."

"Then answer this one," I challenged. "If positive attitudes make us happier, more productive, and more successful, why would anyone in the world choose negativism—a self-inflicted wound—and all the ramifications that come along with that choice? Why would people choose to hurt themselves by being negative?"

"Maybe they choose to be negative because they don't realize they have the power to be positive . . . or perhaps they enjoy feeling sorry for themselves . . . or maybe it's just more difficult to be positive," Tony responded. "Or it could be because negative attitudes are a natural response . . . and some people enjoy it!

"Successful people choose not to inflict the poison of negative attitudes on themselves. Most people love to be around people who are positive and enthusiastic, always looking for the best," he pointed out. "They attract others like a magnet . . . they are the force multiplier. Positive and enthusiastic people add energy to those around them . . . negative and cynical people zap that same energy, draining the room of enthusiasm.

"Jeff, when was the last time you knew a successful person who was consistently described as negative and cynical?"

"I can't think of any off the top of my head," I said. "In fact, the people I know who would be described as negative and cynical are not the people anyone wants to be around."

Tony was nodding. "I feel the same way. In my years of experience, I cannot name one successful person described as negative. Not one. Coincidental? I don't think so. Optimism and enthusiasm are two traits that you will find in most top employees and leaders, regardless of industry, profession, or age.

"Successful people cultivate the habit of enthusiasm in the same way as others cultivate the habit of waking early or exercising. It takes time, perseverance, planning, and commitment," Tony said.

"The power of enthusiasm is evidenced by the effect it has on other people. I remember when, as a kid, you had a positive effect on me. I loved seeing you come around my house because of your enthusiasm. Do you remember selling candy up and down our street for your scout troop?

"Sure, I was the best," I said, abandoning my usual decorum. "I always outsold everyone else and accomplished my goals . . . and besides, it was fun selling to the rich guys like you."

Tony chuckled. "When you came around, I gladly bought from you because you were enthusiastic, loved your product, and enjoyed achieving your goal. I was happy to buy from you and always bought a lot more than I needed.

"I also remember other kids from your troop who came to my house selling the same candy. The difference was that they were trying to sell candy because that is what they had to do. There was no passion, enthusiasm, or energy. The candy was the same, I was the same customer, yet I didn't buy nearly as much from them as I did from you. Their missing ingredient was enthusiasm.

"Real enthusiasm and a positive attitude are not things you put on or take off to fit the occasion or to impress people. Real enthusiasm is a way of life," he pointed out. "Yet many people allow conditions to control their attitude rather than allowing their attitude to help control conditions."

Tony had my attention.

"Enthusiasm is more important to your success than how you dress, how you look, how much skill you have, how much education you've accumulated, and how gifted you think you are.

"The good news is that we have an opportunity to choose the attitude we will have for each situation every day, whether it is a change in job assignments, the way we spend our lunch hour, or our attitude while we're in the car, driving to work.

"All too often we may want to blame our attitude about something on past events and experiences in our lives. Charles

Dickens once advised, 'Reflect upon your present blessings, of which every man has many—not on your past misfortunes, of which all men have some.' Don't brood over mistakes, carry grudges, or harbor hate; each of those negative emotions possesses the power to prevent you from accomplishing the success you desire.

"Jeff, it's easy to have a positive attitude when things are going well. But, unfortunately, life is full of times when things do not work the way we plan and then we arrive at the point at which you were where we began our Monday meetings. You were facing adversity you didn't know how to deal with. You had the courage to do something about it before it was too late, but a lot of people allow adversity literally to consume their thoughts, actions, and enthusiasm."

I nodded in agreement.

"A couple of weeks ago, I was in a meeting of twenty highly successful people, and the topic of adversity was discussed. Every single person agreed that overcoming personal or professional adversity was a critical turning point in their success.

"Think about that. Adversity turned them toward success.

"Within that group, our team had faced cancer, suicide, divorce, loss of children, drug abuse, loss of spouse, significant health issues, loss of jobs, bankruptcy, and other major areas of disappointments. Everyone there had faced a major crisis.

"Successful people have problems just like everyone else. Sometimes adversities are beyond anyone's control, and some are self-inflicted, but regardless of how the adversity

arrived, every successful person has faced, attacked, and conquered adversity somewhere along the way.

"Some say adversity grinds you down. Others say it pol-
ishes you up . . . it depends on what you're made of and how
you choose to attack the adversity that comes your way.

"Of course, it is human nature to dislike adversity,"
Tony continued. "Working through adversity is hard, but
these people can attest that the adversity they were facing
polished them up to become more successful.

"I am firmly convinced that one of the major differ-
ences between successful people and average people is that
successful people make a conscious choice to spend their
energy attacking their situation and moving forward. That
choice is powerful!

"When confronted with adversity, we can choose to see
the positive alternatives and rise from the ashes to become even
better than we were before—or we can choose to sit and savor
our pitiful circumstances for the rest of our lives," Tony said.

I had known people who had done just that. It was
painful, just to remember them.

My mentor continued. "Average people choose to spend
their energy complaining, justifying, and blaming others for
the problem, which changes nothing, much less creates a positive outcome. In fact, complaining drains the energy needed
to begin working their way through the adversity.

"But regardless of how bleak the situation appears, and
I know this from personal experience," Tony said, "there are
alternatives that will help you move forward . . . if you
choose to see them.

"One of the greatest dangers in facing adversity is that we panic, freeze, and stop moving forward because we perceive the roadblocks, barriers, or mountains as insurmountable. But we also know—from the research and our personal experience—that people respond better to crisis when they maximize their forward motion and keep moving. Whatever's happening in your world, when you invest yourself in working toward a goal, there is no time to think about the hurdles. You just keep moving.

"Do you think your past has created a 'natural negative attitude'?" Tony wanted to know. "Unfortunately, we cannot change our past . . . or the fact that people act in a certain way. Remember, your attitude is not externally controlled . . . it is *internally* controlled. If we have a negative attitude, it's because we've made the choice to have that negative attitude at that moment.

"The bottom line is that success is not dependent upon what happens to us . . . success is dependent upon how we react to what happens," Tony said, "and fortunately, optimism can be learned and developed . . . it is your choice. You can choose how you react to events and challenges and become the architect of your own happiness."

Tony paused to let his point soak in, but I was still not sure, specifically, what I could do to improve. "Tony, you have spent as much time on this subject as you have on the topics of any of our other meetings. Obviously, you must think it is important and an area in which I could use some improvement, but I am not sure what I can do to be a more optimistic and enthusiastic person."

As usual, Tony had a lesson up his proverbial sleeve. "You're right. I do think this is a critical area for your personal and professional success, and I've been eagerly awaiting this meeting to pass on to you some of my father's wisdom.

"One of the lessons he taught me was what he called the Six Laws of Growing Optimism."

He stood up and retrieved a note from his file. "This is my father's handwriting. He gave it to me over thirty years ago . . . and nothing has changed."

1. You Reap Only What You Sow—If you've sown apple seeds, you'll get apples. Don't expect oaks from apple seeds. If you want to be more optimistic, sow seeds of optimism. Sow positive behaviors to reap positive results.

2. Know Where to Sow—Seeds sown on rocks will never bear fruit. Find fertile ground and sow your seeds there. Commit to positive projects, people, and tasks. Spend your energies to achieve positive goals, never wasting precious resources.

3. When the Time Is Right, Reap—One farmer loved to cultivate and till the soil into neat rows and then sow his seed, but when it came time for harvest, he hated to drive the combine into the fields, crushing the neat mounds of soil and leaving nothing but chaff in its wake. If we sow, if we make the effort, then we must reap. Otherwise, why bother?

4. We Can't Do Anything About Last Year's Harvest—Life is filled with important choices, and

every choice has a consequence. It's not about whether last year's harvest was good or bad. It's about how we handled the success or failure of that harvest. Did our failure prevent us from sowing positive seeds today? We can do something about only this year's crop . . . but we can also take what we learned last year and make this year's harvest more bountiful.

5. Don't Worry About the Weather—or Anything Else. Worry is a wasted effort and the breeding ground of doubt. It will lead you to focus on potential losses rather than effective solutions. Your best choice to stop worry is to take positive actions that will prevent the worry from happening.

6. Be Easy on Yourself—It's important to have the strength and the desire to continue sowing. Beating yourself up for a poor harvest only wastes time. You can never like anyone else more than you like yourself—and don't expect others to like you if you don't hold yourself in high esteem.

He folded the piece of paper. "I am still amazed by my dad's wisdom," Tony said.

"He did not have all of the resources we have today. He never experienced the speed of life we have, yet as you could see on this paper, he knew the timeless requirement for success was optimism. My dad was right: enthusiasm and optimism are definitely our choices—the right choice for those who seek a successful career."

As he paused, I savored this moment with Tony . . . and I was grateful for his generosity once again.

"I feel like this session has been a lecture so far," Tony continued, "but I needed to hear myself say some of those things because, like you, I am facing some challenges where I have to work on keeping a positive attitude. So thanks for listening to me talk to myself as I was talking to you."

"It was good for me to hear as well." I acknowledged. "Needless to say, I have fallen into the trap of allowing my past to consume my future and, at minimum, I will be much more aware of the power of my attitude.

"Having a positive attitude as an adult is not as natural as it was when I was selling candy for my scout troop . . . there are a lot more pressures, and sometimes I really have to work and make a conscious effort to be enthusiastic.

"What I can I commit to you is that your words . . . and your dad's wisdom . . . will be a part of my legacy that I leave with others."

"Great!" Tony said. "And speaking of legacy, I think it is appropriate to end our sessions talking about the gift of your legacy."

Tony smiled and quickly zoomed into what seemed to be an odd question. "Did you see the movie *Groundhog Day*—the one in which Bill Murray lives the same day over and over again?"

"Yes, pretty funny movie," I said.

"Well, that's the way many people live their lives," Tony explained. "They wake up and do the same things over and over and over—because that's what they're comfortable doing—until it's time to retire. They make no effort to leave behind something that will last long past their days.

"Jeff, you have too much potential to be living *Groundhog Day* over and over, which helps me make my next point. A forceful enemy to your potential is your comfort zone. When you first came to my home ten weeks ago, without knowing it, you described what it was like to be in your comfort zone. Then, things changed at work and your comfort zone was no longer comfortable; you didn't know what to do or where to go. You probably felt frustrated and panicked at the same time.

"For you to be the very best, you cannot allow yourself to become complacent in your comfort zone. You need to continually reach for improvement. To fulfill your potential, you need to move out of your comfort zone and into the 'legacy zone.'"

"The legacy zone?" I repeated.

"I want you to think for a minute and then answer these two questions: What does legacy mean to you, and what kind of legacy would you like to create?"

After pausing for a minute, I replied, "To me, legacy is a gift that I leave for someone—sort of like a hand-me-down. The legacy I would like to create and hand down would be that I gave 100 percent in everything I did and helped others become better."

"That's great," Tony responded. "In other words, your legacy would be that you did your very best and gave knowledge and experience to others?"

"Right. You said it better than me, but the bottom line is that I want to make a difference."

"Jeff, if you really want to give a 100 percent, make a difference, and leave a lasting legacy, you will be one of the very few people who actually accomplish that goal.

"Andrew Carnegie once said, 'The average person puts only 25 percent of his energy and ability into his work. The world takes off its hat to those who put in more than 50 percent of their capacity and stands on its head for those few and far between souls who devote 100 percent.'

"What a shame! *You* have too much talent to be average. I hope you will make the choice to be one of the few and far between souls who gives everything he has to become successful and then gives away everything he has learned. If for no other reason, do it selfishly; in order to get more, you must give more," Tony explained. "It is the generous giving of our knowledge that produces our legacy."

"Becoming successful is hard work and takes its toll. We all lose our spirit, and our inner fire is quenched by things that happen in our life. That is what brought you here ten weeks ago. Your inner fire was almost out—barely a flicker. You needed someone to rekindle the fire, and only another human being can help at that time. I am thankful you chose me to work with you to fan the small flicker and allow it to flame again.

"Think about what would happen if there were no people willing to share their knowledge and experiences with others. Our society would be stymied. There would be no positive role models, no examples, no endowments, no helping hands, no help for the homeless, no voice for the voiceless.

"Consider it. Without people like you choosing to give your knowledge back, we would not have the wealth of past experience to call upon, the wisdom to look beyond the horizon for the next strategy or direction. Your decision to leave a legacy will live on long after your last breath.

"But how do we—in this day and time—really feel about this legacy of giving?" Tony wanted to know. "Are we put here to give a bit of ourselves to others? Are we defined by what we give? Why should we choose to give?"

"I think we should choose to give because it is the right thing to do," I said. "But it is pretty difficult to make the effort to give while most of us are just trying to survive."

"Without a doubt, it takes a lot of endurance to put other people first, particularly when the people we are giving to are often so preoccupied with themselves that they don't seem to notice our efforts," my mentor continued. "And—as you said—our schedules are normally full, even before we start giving our time and energy to others."

"George Washington Carver once said, 'How far you go in life depends on you being tender with the young, compassionate with the aged, sympathetic with the striving, and tolerant of the weak and the strong. Because someday in life you will have been all of these.'

"The joy of your legacy is in the gift you give, not in what you receive in return," Tony pointed out. "The purpose of giving is not to receive back in full measure. If you give solely with the expectation of receiving something in return, prepare to be disappointed. After all, if expecting something in return is your reason for giving, you are really not giving—you're swapping. If you receive something in return for your gift, what you receive is a bonus—not a repayment of debt."

"Tony, I am not sure I have much to give. I am still trying to survive every day and have not reached the pinnacle of success that you and others who leave a true legacy have reached."

"If you wait until you have achieved your definition of success, you will miss out on the joy of legacy," Tony said. "Only your time and wisdom are required to build a legacy.

"Start with the person who sits next to you at work—your peer, your boss, or just an acquaintance. Start somewhere. You never know where you will make a difference that will change a person's life.

"Giving of ourselves should come from the heart—and, without fail, when this kind of giving happens, we are generously repaid for every kindness we share," Tony said with a smile. "And most of the time, we never know the impact of our gift.

"There is a legendary story about a farmer who discovered a young boy stuck in a mud bog somewhere in the United Kingdom. After much struggle, the farmer was finally able to free the lad, although for a moment the farmer felt that he, too, would sink too deeply into the mud to survive. Later that evening, a lord stopped by the farmer's humble shanty, identifying himself as the rescued boy's father and offering to pay him a generous reward for his effort.

"When the farmer refused, the lord saw that the farmer had a son and insisted that he pay the boy's way to college. After the farmer's son graduated with a degree in science, the young man—Alexander Fleming—went on to discover penicillin. Ironically, the young man who had been rescued from the bog, now a young adult, came down with pneumonia.

Thanks to Fleming's discovery—penicillin—his life was saved. That young man's name: Sir Winston Churchill.

"Whether this tale is true or a mix of myth and legend, its moral easily reflects life—what we do for others eventually comes back to us multiplied. It's the law of legacy.

"There are people all around you today who could use your experience, advice, and counsel," Tony said. "Just look around . . . people are desperate for help and do not know where to go or who to turn to. You may have the experience to make a profound difference in their life just by taking the time to offer your experience.

"Once there was a man walking down the street who fell into a hole. The hole was so deep, he could not escape. He looked in all directions and could not figure out how to raise himself from the hole.

"A preacher walked by, heard the man's cry for help, and inquired, 'Why are you in that hole in the road?' The man replied: 'I fell in and I can't get out.' The preacher said that he would pray for him and walked away.

"A police officer walked by, heard the man's cry for help, and inquired, 'Why are you in that hole in the road?' The man replied: 'I fell in and I can't get out.' The policeman said it was against the law to be in a hole in the road, wrote him a ticket, threw it into the hole, and walked away.

"An environmentalist walked by, heard the man's cry for help, and inquired, 'Why are you in that hole in the road?' The man replied, 'I fell in and I can't get out.' The environmentalist said it was environmentally unsafe to be in a hole in the road and began to picket, circling the hole and holding a sign reading, 'Man in Hole in Road . . . Environmentally Unsafe!'

"Another person walked by, heard the man's cry for help, and inquired, 'Why are you in that hole in the road?' The man replied, 'I fell in and I can't get out.' Without hesitation, the unknown man jumped into the hole with him.

"The man in the hole said, 'Why did you jump in this hole? I can't get out. I have had a preacher praying for me, a policeman writing me a ticket, and this goofy person picketing outside . . . and you chose to jump down here with me. Are you crazy? Why would you jump down here with me?'

"The unknown man replied, 'Don't worry. I chose to jump in this hole with you because I have been in this hole before, and I know the way out!'

"Jeff, maybe you have not faced the exact same situation that has led to rescuing someone in a 'deep hole.' Nevertheless, you can listen to, coach, and support those who are working their way out of the holes they have fallen into. Trusted counselors, mentors, and guides make an indelible mark on the lives they touch, and they provide the two ingredients to success in life—caring and sharing—that cannot be learned or purchased," Tony pointed out.

"More than ever, people today need positive role models, and there is an abundance of role models—but there is a scarcity of positive role models. You see, wherever you are, whatever you do, you are a role model for everyone who sees you. The choice that you have to make is which role you will model—one of positive influence or not.

"What you do with your life will be your legacy. No one requires you to make a contribution. It is something you do to help someone along the way, to support your colleagues, your friends and those whom you may not know.

It is a gift that comes without a price tag. Your legacy is priceless.

"You may be successful, but your choice to leave a legacy by giving of yourself distinguishes you most, providing the greatest meaning to your life because your example will live into the next generation through the lives you touch," Tony concluded.

"Tony, this is our last meeting for a while. I do want to begin my legacy right now. How did you get started being a mentor for others? Is there a path that I can follow? Where do I start?"

"Your legacy begins when you decide to leave your comfort zone and enter into what I call the legacy zone," Tony said. "Let me explain. To leave a legacy, you have to have knowledge to share. To obtain that knowledge you have to do things differently than others.

"There are three rooms in the legacy zone," he explained. "The first room is the reading room. Look around this library—there are more than a thousand books in here. More than half of those books are about management and leadership. Executives call me to help them solve business problems. I've never 'made up' a solution. None of their problems are unique. The value I offer is the wisdom of all the people who have written these books.

"You learn more by reading more. I'm living proof that the more you learn, the more you earn. Do you think it is coincidental that, in most cases, the bigger the house, the bigger the library inside the house? Leaving a legacy requires continuing to increase your knowledge so that you will have more knowledge to give away."

I looked around the room, suddenly overwhelmed by the knowledge and wisdom on the shelves that surrounded us.

"Did you know most people don't read one nonfiction book in a year? Not one," Tony said incredulously. "You'd think books were scarce or expensive. But there is an abundance of books at every public library, waiting for people simply to walk in and check them out—at no charge—free! Many top executives of organizations will read up to ten books a month, yet average American workers will probably not read ten books in their lifetimes."

Tony went on. "There is a direct correlation between the books you read and the success you achieve. Here's a challenge. The next time you visit someone's home, check out the books on the table next to his or her favorite chair. See what kind of books are on the bookshelves. By doing that, you can generally tell what has molded the philosophy and values of that person.

"The good news is that there is an abundance of books available to teach you or inform you about any subject you are interested in.

"Now, let's suppose you decided to read one book a month on management or leadership," he continued. "Most books are between twelve and twenty chapters, so you'd be reading about half a chapter a day, which would take you about ten minutes. During the next year, you'd have read twelve books. Do you think you'd know more about management and leadership if you read twelve books a year on the subject?"

This was a rare no-brainer question for our Monday mornings. "Of course," I said.

"When the next job opening at a higher position in the company comes up, would you be better prepared to assume that role?"

"Of course!"

"See, Jeff, the question is *not* do you have the time or money. The question is do you have the *discipline* to set aside time every day to read," Tony pointed out. "In your case, you probably won't retire for at least fifteen years. In fifteen years, you could read one hundred eighty books just by reading half a chapter a day. Make it a priority to read, and your knowledge will likely make you the obvious choice for the next promotion.

"Charlie Jones, my friend and wise counsel, says, 'You are today what you'll be five years from now, except for the people you meet and the books you read.' Think about that. In five years, you can be completely different or just like you are right now—it is your choice."

Tony wasn't through. "I would not limit myself to just business books. Read things that are interesting to you and provide you knowledge to share. Would you like to sit down and talk to Albert Einstein? Then read one of his essays. What would you like to ask Churchill about his life experiences? Pick up any of hundreds of books and read how he would answer your question. Would you enjoy hearing Ronald Reagan tell how it felt to tell Gorbachev "Tear these walls down!"? Read his memoirs.

"How about listening to Peter Drucker or Jack Welch talk about management and leadership? Read their books. Or if you want to become a more complete thinker, read the Bible, as the vast majority of great thinkers have done, whether they believed it or not.

"You may be limited in the people you will meet in your lifetime," Tony said, "and many of the people we would like to meet and enjoy learning from are not alive or may not be available to us. But you are not limited in what you can learn from others. Reward yourself with the knowledge of great people and become a better person because of the information waiting for you in books.

"Don't stifle your career by limiting your knowledge."

"But, there are so many options," I said. "Where do I start?"

"Where do you start? Anywhere," Tony said. "Just start enjoying the company of the greats or the pleasantness of the interesting by reading! Just get started! The more you learn, the more you will be able to earn and the more information you will have to give. Don't go through a day without reading—it will change your life.

"The second room in the legacy zone is the listening room. Did you know the principle reasons that executives fail are arrogance, out-of-control egos, and insensitivity?

"These executives forget to take the time to listen to their people. Soon they become insensitive to the needs and desires of the individuals on the team. Arrogance, out-of-control egos, and insensitivity are part of the management land trap. Don't allow yourself to fall into that trap—listen to your people!

"I have a few other comments about listening I wanted to share," Tony said before taking a sip of coffee. "First, you tend to listen better when you attend outside seminars and conferences. Any time you gather new information, you can make better decisions.

"Second, you can also learn to listen better by making better use of your time while you're in your car. The average person spends more than five hundred hours per year in his or her car. That's a lot of time. Maybe spending some of that time listening to a motivational or inspirational CD would have a greater influence on your success than listening to talk radio or music. It's just a thought. . . .

"The third room in the legacy zone is the giving room. That is where your legacy actually begins. I strongly feel you cannot succeed without giving back," Tony continued. "There are reasons why hearses don't have luggage racks! Your legacy will be what you leave others.

"When we started these sessions, one of the requirements was that you would have to teach others what I was teaching you," Tony reminded. "My purpose in making that a requirement was so you would become more accountable. The more you teach, the more accountable you become to what you're teaching. Teaching is good for you!

"I realize it's easy to agree we need to become lifelong learners, but the fact is, nothing is going to change unless you set specific goals for improvement.

"You may have heard the story of people who went to the airport to wait for their ship to come in. The only problem is that ships don't arrive at airports! If you want your ship to come in, you've got to go where the ships are. In personal improvement, the ships are in goals—specific, measurable, and obtainable goals.

"I've found that goals can become the strongest force for self-motivation—they are your track to run your course," Tony said. "Yet less than 5 percent of all people set specific goals, and fewer than 5 percent will write their goals down on paper.

"If goals are so important, why don't more people set them?" Tony asked rhetorically. "I think there are four main reasons why people fail to set goals.

"First, people fail to set goals because they don't know the importance of goal setting. Every great accomplishment I know about has begun with a goal written down on a sheet of paper. Achieving the goal is automatic. Setting the goal is the issue.

"Second, most people don't know how to set goals. After each session, I asked you to write down what actions you were going to take the next week. I did that because writing clarifies the goal and commits you to it.

"Third, sometimes people don't set goals because they're afraid of failure. If you have no goals, you're not risking failure. I think we should do the opposite—fail faster and more often. Failure is a prelude to success. To become more successful, we have to fail more often . . . but don't take this to an extreme. I'm talking about setting goals that will help us become more successful even if we fail to accomplish the goal.

"Fourth, goals require people to leave their comfort zone. That can be scary for many people because it often involves having to learn new skills.

"But, Jeff, nothing would please me more than to watch you become a fantastic goal setter and goal achiever. You can become a leader who has balance in his life. You can become a great role model for others to follow. But over the years, I've learned that most people don't want to follow someone who loses his health or his family because he works all the time. People want to follow someone who is balanced in all areas, not just work.

"My final thought for you is this: Stay positive! Of course you will become discouraged again somewhere along the way. Just don't give up. This world is not for Pollyannas. Bad things happen to even the best people.

"You know how much I enjoy golf. Well, I think golf is a great teacher of life's lessons as well as leadership lessons, and I've learned that in every round of golf, at least three bad things are going to happen that are not deserved:

"You may hit the ball in the middle of the fairway only to discover the ball in an old divot. Or you hit the perfect shot right before the wind gusts and your shot lands just short, buried in the bunker. Or perhaps your perfect putt moves off course because someone didn't take time to fix their ball mark. None of those bad breaks were deserved, and all of them seem unfair at the time. The mark of a great golfer is taking whatever break—good or bad—comes his way and making a positive move forward.

"Similar unfair things happen in business. The question is not, Are unfair things going to happen? The question is, How are you going to react to whatever happens? Ultimately, your true measure of success is being able to look in the mirror and know that you had the courage to do what you thought was right."

Like always, Tony made good points, too good to forget, so I was busily writing down almost everything he said.

"So much of life is about attitude and how we handle what life throws our way," Tony said. "Life is good—even when a situation appears to be the worst. Stay positive and help make another's life better!

"Winston Churchill once said, 'To every man there comes in his lifetime that special moment when he is tapped on the shoulder and offered the chance to do a very special thing. What a tragedy if that moment finds him unprepared or unqualified for the work which would be his finest hour.'

"During these past ten weeks I have passed to you the knowledge that has been passed to me to prepare you for your finest hour, and so once again, Jeff, we are about out of time. For the last time, I'll ask my question: What are you going to do differently?"

"Well, Tony, I think you saved your best lessons for last. I suspected you would ask me what I would do differently one more time, so I came prepared. I've reviewed my notes from all the previous sessions, and here are my commitments:

Jeff's Leadership Commitments

I am responsible for my actions and my team's performance, no matter what the circumstances.

I am willing to pay the price to get past splat.

I keep the main thing the main thing.

I have a positive relationship with my boss.

---

*I escape from management land and stay in
tune with my people.*

---

*I value feedback and make adjustments based
on constructive criticism.*

I recognize and reward superstar activity.

I address problems in a pro-active manner.

I do what's right even when no one is watching.

---

*I realize that everything I do counts toward my
leadership score.*

I hire tough.

---

*I proactively work through exits to get
to the opportunities awaiting me in new
entrances.*

I am an excellent time manager.

I fill other's buckets.

"And after this week's session, I'm going to add several more:

I do not let my past consume my future.

I am an enthusiastic leader.

――――――――――――――

I will be easy on myself and everyone else. We are all works in progress.

――――――――――――――

I begin my legacy right now.

――――――――――――――

I am a positive role model for others.

"Wonderful, Jeff! My, you have come a long way in the past ten weeks," Tony said, standing and shaking my hand.

I was feeling proud and even emotional, but it was meaningful that my mentor had so much faith in me. "Before I leave, I have something for you in my car," I said. "I'll be right back."

When I returned, I handed Tony a gift-wrapped box. "Here, this is for you," I said.

Tony opened the present—a big brass bucket with his initials engraved on the front. It was filled to overflowing with thirty or so small gifts.

"At the risk of sounding corny, this gift represents what you have done for me the past ten weeks," I explained, a lump beginning in my throat. "You filled my bucket with your gifts of insight, wisdom, and your own personal legacy. I hope that every time you see one of these small gifts around your home, you will think of the time that we were able to spend together. I will never forget our Monday Morning Meetings.

"So my question to you is, When can we meet again?"

"I want to take your family out to dinner soon." Tony replied. "But, as far as our lessons, remember—when we began our sessions, you committed to teach others what I would be teaching you. When you do that, then we'll get together.

"Thank you for the bucket and gifts, Jeff. I am honored you called me and allowed me to share my experiences with you. I learned a lot from you during our sessions. Just remember to take what you have learned and pass it on."

I took a deep breath as I walked outside and turned to wave. "So long, Tony. See you soon!"

The Gift of Your Legacy

Don't let my past consume my future.

Get out of my comfort zone and begin my legacy zone.

Read every day.

Set goals.

Stay positive.

Epilogue

Present day . . .

My ten Monday Morning meetings with Tony served as the turning point in my career. His gentle wisdom has guided my actions and my path during the past two years.

Six months ago I was promoted, and Jeni, who left our company and then came back, took over my old position. I am enjoying my new position, and I am mentoring two people each week sharing Tony's wisdom. Tony was right—I keep my bucket full by sharing my knowledge and experience.

Tony's mentoring improved my family life as well as my career.

I discovered that his lessons transferred well into my personal life. I did a self-evaluation on why I was struggling at home and found many of the same issues applied—I did not keep the main thing the main thing, my communication with my family was inconsistent, my personal time management was not productive, and I was allowing some things that happened in the past to consume my present and future. Now I try to fill a lot more buckets around the house.

Most people don't have—and will never have—the luxury of a mentor like Tony. My desire is that you will be able to learn from him and pass on this knowledge to others.

Now I can make my call to Tony to set up our next meeting. . . .

Wisdom from Tony

A Collection of Quotations

"When it comes to leading people, there is no problem that is unique to you."

"Successful people keep moving, even when they are discouraged and have made mistakes."

"We all need people who will help us look at situations from a different perspective."

"Even though your responsibilities increase when you become a manager, you lose some of the rights or freedoms you may have enjoyed in the past."

"A real leader spends his time fixing the problem instead of finding who to blame."

"When you accepted your job, you were not chosen solely to fill a position on the organization chart; you were chosen to fill a responsibility."

"I have found success is ultimately realized by people who make more right

choices . . . and recover quickly from their
bad choices."

"When you write things down, you commit to
doing them. If you simply tell me what you want
to do, there is really no commitment to getting
it done."

"There is no 'grand conspiracy' preventing
you from accomplishing what you need
to do."

"When you depend on another's perceptions to
match your expectations, you're setting yourself
up for disappointment."

"People quit people before they quit companies."

"For you to be successful and provide your
employees with the necessary tools for success,
you and your boss must work together—no
matter what."

"Take the time and energy to manage your
boss the same way you manage
your team."

"One of the main things for a leader is to
eliminate confusion."

"If your focus is always changing, expect confusion to be rampant on your team."

"You have to escape from management land and get in touch with your people."

"Your job is not to lower the bottom by adjusting for and accommodating the lowest-performing employees. You should be raising the top by recognizing and rewarding superstar behaviors!"

"The worst type of employee you can have is one who has mentally quit and is still physically coming to work every day."

"The single greatest demotivator of a team is having members who are not carrying their load."

"It is rare for people to say they want to be held accountable, but in reality, everyone wants everyone else to be held accountable."

"Doing the right thing isn't always easy—in fact, sometimes it's real hard—but just remember that doing the right thing is always right."

"The truth is that problems won't just go away."

"Leaders who have integrity possess one of the most respected virtues in all of life."

"Everything you do matters because your team is watching . . . and depending on you to do the right thing."

"Guard your integrity as if it's your most precious leadership possession, because that is what it is."

"The most important thing you do as a leader is to hire the right people."

"What you see in the interview will not get significantly better when the individual is hired."

"Never lower your standards just to fill a position. You will pay for it later."

"The success of any change depends, in large measure, on your attitude about that change."

"You can help determine your team's enthusiasm for the change by focusing on the entrance of potential while you are working through the exit of the past."

"One of the major sources of stress, anxiety, and unhappiness comes from feeling as if your life is out of control."

————————

"If you want to make better use of your time, you need to be looking for the small increments of time . . . a minute here, five minutes there, et cetera."

————————

"There are a few things that you can do that will yield better results than doing a whole lot of other things."

————————

"You will never have enough time to do everything you need to do, so what you need is a crystal clear understanding of the important things you have to do."

————————

"You are the chief bucket filler, and the best way to fill buckets is with excellent communication."

————————

"Your team has entrusted a portion of their life to you, and it's your job to help them grow, personally and professionally."

————————

"Bucket filling is in the eye of the bucket holder, not the bucket filler. Fill their buckets with things that are important to them . . . not you."

————————

"Enthusiasm is something you can't fake, and it has a tremendous effect on everyone around you."

"If you want to be around people who are positive and enthusiastic and eager to live life, your attitude has to be the same."

"Every successful person has faced, attacked, and conquered adversity somewhere along the way."

"To fulfill your potential, you need to move out of your comfort zone and into the legacy zone."

"Give away everything you have learned. If for no other reason, do it selfishly; in order to get more, you must give more."

"There is a direct correlation between the books you read and the success you achieve."

"Don't stifle your career by limiting your knowledge."

"So much of life is about attitude and how we handle what life throws our way. Life is good— even when a situation appears to be the worst."

Acknowledgments

Over the years, I have been blessed with some wonderful mentors. My success has been molded and formed by those who always seem to have the time to listen and the wisdom to share.

I thank the following people for being my mentors:

Alice Adams, Ken Carnes, Lee Colan, Eric Harvey, Charlie "Tremendous" Jones, Louis Kruger, Mark Layton, Joe Miles, Tony Van Roekel, and Tod Taylor.

I am also grateful for the people whose concepts generated ideas for lessons in this book: Keep the Main Thing the Main Thing—Jim Barksdale, former COO at FedEx; The 'Do Right' Rule—my dad, who always questioned, 'What is the right thing'; Hire Tough—my friend Eric Harvey; Exits and Entrances—my pastor, Glen Schmucker; and Buckets and Dippers—the late Don Clifton, from the Gallup Organization.

I thank the team who have made CornerStone a success beyond anyone's belief: Alice Adams, Barbara Bartlett, Jim Garner, Harry Hopkins, and Melissa Monogue.

I am especially thankful for David Hale Smith, my brilliant, creative agent, and for my talented editor, Marion Maneker, and his entire HarperCollins team, who were a valuable source of expertise and encouragement.

To all of you whom I have named, please accept my deepest thanks.

To each person who reads this book, best wishes as you become a positive role model, mentor, and friend for the people around you.

About the Author

David Cottrell, president and CEO of CornerStone Leadership Institute, is an internationally known leadership consultant, educator, and speaker. His business experience includes leadership positions with Xerox and FedEx. He also led the successful turnaround of a Chapter 11 company before founding CornerStone.

The author of twenty books, including *Listen Up; Leader, The Next Level: Leadership Beyond the Status Quo; Monday Morning Leadership; Leadership . . . Biblically Speaking; Management Insights; Leadership Courage; and Birdies, Pars, and Bogeys: Leadership Lessons from the Links.*

David is a thought-provoking and electrifying professional speaker. He has presented his leadership message to more than 125,000 managers worldwide. His powerful wisdom and insights on leadership have made him a highly

sought after keynote speaker and seminar leader as well as a
featured leadership expert on public television.

He and his wife, Karen, reside in Horseshoe Bay, Texas.
David can be reached at
www.CornerStoneLeadership.com.

Five Ways to Bring Monday Morning Mentoring into Your Organization

Monday Morning Mentoring PowerPoint Presentation

Introduce and reinforce the Monday Morning Mentoring to your organization with this complete and cost-effective presentation. All of the main concepts and ideas in the book are reinforced in this professionally produced, downloadable PowerPoint presentation with facilitator guide and notes. $99.95. Download at www.CornerStoneLeadership.com.

Keynote Presentation

Invite author David Cottrell to inspire your team and help create greater success for your organization. Each

presentation is designed to set a solid foundation for both organizational and personal success.

Monday Morning Mentoring Workshop

Facilitated by David Cottrell or a certified CornerStone
Leadership instructor, this three- or six-hour workshop will
reinforce the principles of Monday Morning Mentoring, and
each participant will develop a personal action plan that can
make a profound difference in his or her life and career.

Monday Morning Mentoring Profile

This online profile assesses your personal strengths and
provides insight to gaps that may be preventing your success.
It provides the framework to create an actionable develop-
ment plan leveraging the concepts of Monday Morning
Mentoring.

Monday Morning Mentoring Audio CD

Available at *www.CornerStoneLeadership.com* or call
888-789-LEAD (5323)